MARKETING NUTRITION

MARKETING NUTRITION

Soy, Functional Foods, Biotechnology, and Obesity

BRIAN WANSINK

UNIVERSITY OF ILLINOIS PRESS
URBANA AND CHICAGO

♾ This book is printed on acid-free paper.

The Library of Congress cataloged the cloth edition as follows:
Wansink, Brian.
Marketing nutrition : soy, functional foods, biotechnology,
and obesity
p. cm. — (The food series)
Includes bibliographical references and index.
ISBN 0-252-02942-9 (cloth : alk. paper)
ISBN 978-0-252-02942-4 (cloth : alk. paper)
1. Communication in diet therapy. 2. Patient education.
3. Food habits. 4. Nutrition. [DNLM: 1. Marketing. 2. Nutrition.
3. Consumer Satisfaction—economics. 4. Food Industry—
economics. QU 145 W251m 2004] I. Title. II. Series.
RM214.3.W36   2004
615.8'54—dc22   2004002526

PAPERBACK ISBN 0-252-07455-6 / 978-0-252-07455-4

To my loving parents, John and Naomi Wansink,
who taught me all that is genuine and nutritious in food and in life

Contents

PART 5: MARKETING NUTRITION

Acknowledgments

Many of the insights in this book emerged from research projects by far-sighted funding groups such as the National Soybean Research Lab (NSRL) and the Soy Foods Center at the University of Illinois, the Council for Agricultural Research (C-FAR), the Illinois-Missouri Biotechnology Alliance (IMBA), the Illinois Attorney General, and the Illinois Soybean Program Operating Board. Most of these projects were done in conjunction with some of the most interesting, stimulating, witty people I have known, including Steve Sonka, Pierre Chandon, Joost Pennings, Se-Bum Park, Koert van Ittersum, James Painter, Junyong Kim, Randy Westgren, Peter Goldsmith, Mike Mazzaco, and Claire Hasler.

I thank the researchers in my Food and Brand Lab at the University of Illinois. Their selfless "get it to me over the weekend" help in critiquing the chapters and providing additional ideas represents the ethos that makes Illinois a world-class university. The "Brand Labbers" who have been involved in *Marketing Nutrition* include Herb Jackson, Matthew Cheney, Sarah Jo Brenner, Nilguen Eren, Jorge Chirboga, Jill North, Eduardo Baez, and Greg Szymack. In addition, thanks to my colleagues Jeff Schmidt and especially Koert van Ittersum for providing valuable suggestions and wisdom during the process.

Two people stand out as a critical part of this book. The first is fellow Iowa native Steve Sonka, who helped bring me to Illinois in 1997 and whose words of support and advice over the past seven years have always been wise and witty. The second is my Cordon Bleu nutritional gatekeeper, Jennifer, whose meals sustained me as I wrote this book.

Credits

Portions of Chapter 2 were adopted from an earlier article in the *Journal of Public Policy and Marketing* and republished with permission of the American Marketing Association. The full citation of the article is: Wansink, Brian (2002), "Changing Eating Habits on the Home Front: Lost Lessons from World War II Research," *Journal of Public Policy and Marketing*, 21:1 (Spring), 90–99.

Portions of Chapter 3 were adopted from an earlier article in the *Cornell Hotel and Restaurant Administrative Quarterly* and republished with permission of Sage Publications, Inc. The full citation of the article is: Wansink, Brian, James M. Painter, and Koert van Ittersum, (2001) "Descriptive Menu Labels' Effect on Sales," *Cornell Hotel and Restaurant Administrative Quarterly*, 42:6 (December), 68–72.

Portions of Chapter 5 were adopted from an earlier article in *Qualitative Market Research* and republished with permission of Emerald Group Publishing Limited. The referenced article is: "Using Laddering to Understand and Leverage a Brand's Equity," Wansink, Brian—*Qualitative Market Research* (2003, Vol.6, No.2).

Portions of Chapter 6 are reprinted from *Food Quality and Preference*, 14:4 (June), Brian Wansink, "Profiling Nutritional Gatekeepers: Three Methods for Differentiating Influential Cooks," 289–97, 2003, with permission from Elsevier.

Portions of Chapter 9 were adopted from an earlier article in the *American Behavioral Scientist* and republished with permission of Sage Publications, Inc. The full citation of the article is: Wansink, Brian and Junyong Kim (2001). "The Marketing Battle Over Genetically Modified Foods: False Assumptions about Consumer Behavior," *American Behavioral Scientist*, 44:8 (April), 1405–17.

Portions of Chapter 10 were adopted from an earlier article in the *Advances in Food and Nutrition Research* and republished with permission of Emerald Group Publishing Limited. The referenced article is: "Consumer Reactions to Food Safety Crises," Wansink, Brian—*Advances in Food and Nutrition Research,* (2004, Vol. 48, 103–50).

Portions of Chapter 12 were adopted from an earlier article in the *Journal of Consumer Affairs* and republished with permission of Sage Publishing, Inc. The full citation of the article is: Wansink, Brian (2003), "How Do Front and Back Package Labels Influence Beliefs About Health Claims?" *Journal of Consumer Affairs,* 37:2 (Winter), 305–16.

Portions of Chapter 13 were adopted from an earlier article in the *Review of Agricultural Economics* and republished with permission of Blackwell Publishing. The full citation of the article is: Wansink, Brian, Steven T. Sonka, and Matthew M. Cheney (2002), "A Cultural Hedonic Framework for Increasing the Consumption of Unfamiliar Foods: Soy Acceptance in Russia and Columbia," *Review of Agricultural Economics,* 24:2, 353–65.

Portions of Chapter 14 were adopted from an earlier article in *Journal of International Food and Agribusiness Marketing* and republished with permission of Haworth Press, Inc. The full citation of the article is: Wansink, Brian, Steven Sonka, Peter Goldsmith, Jorge Chiriboga, and Nilgün Eren (2004), "Increasing the Acceptance of Soy-Based Foods," *Journal of International Food and Agribusiness Marketing,* 16:1, 74–94.

MARKETING NUTRITION

Introduction

Marketing is not simply a clever "Got Milk" advertising campaign, a fifty-cent coupon on a soy burger, or a convenient combination pack of precut vegetables. In the context of nutrition, marketing is much broader. It focuses on all efforts to encourage and enable people to eat more nutritiously. Many people involved in marketing might call it education, public service, or simply good parenting. Sometimes it takes the form of education programs or innovative distribution programs; sometimes it takes the form of more direct efforts. Marketing encompasses the following types of decisions:

- A dietitian is thinking how to best motivate a recovering patient to maintain a high-fiber diet after surgery.
- A food administrator is trying to determine how to best teach food aid recipients in a developing country how to use protein-rich grains in new recipes.
- A brand manager is trying to determine what information to highlight on the label of his product and whether to distribute it through health food stores or through mass market channels.

Each of these people is addressing a marketing-related challenge that involves encouraging others to change from less nutritious eating patterns to more nutritious ones. This is not unlike what happens when a mother tries to encourage her children to eat carrots by shredding them and putting them into orange Jell-O. Although simple in concept, this becomes much more difficult to execute the farther we move from shredded carrots at the dinner table. Part of this difficulty can be attributed to some of the well-meaning but misguided perspectives that are brought to nutrition marketing.

Four Misguided Perspectives of Nutrition Marketing

Despite the tremendous importance of nutrition, efforts to encourage the consumption of nutritious foods have been surprisingly ineffective. This is often because these efforts are directed by talented people who have the right intentions but the wrong experiences. Their hearts are in the right place, but their experience is not. Consider four perspectives from four different people: a dietitian, a government administrator, a marketing manager, and a researcher.

The "Nutritional Knowledge Is Power" Perspective: Dietitian

Sometimes it is assumed that once people know that food is nutritious, they will want to eat it. These efforts have been generally unsuccessful in the same way that knowing that doing fifty situps every morning is good for us does not motivate many of us to do these fifty situps. The "nutritional knowledge is power" perspective is the approach of many well-meaning nutrition experts and dietitians. Their intimacy with nutritional knowledge leads them to believe that simply passing on this knowledge is all that is necessary to induce change. After delivering their message of health, some believe that their work is done. Unfortunately, many people will not eat any better even if we can get them to pass a nutrition quiz.

Figure I.1 illustrates that less than 20 percent of the population is actively trying to reduce their intake of sugar, fats, oils, red meat, and junk food. It is doubtful that they believe these are good for them to eat, yet they continue to do so.

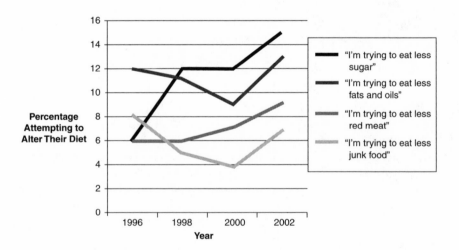

Figure I.1. Priorities in eating more nutritiously. (Food Marketing Institute 2002.)

The "Food Aid Is Food Eaten" Perspective: Government Administrator

A second approach to marketing nutrition or encouraging a change in eating behavior assumes that desperate people resort to desperate measures. This is akin to assuming that if people are starving, dumping a bargeload of grain in front of them will guarantee that they will eat it. Perhaps this is true under such extreme circumstances.

Yet for developed countries, most work in nutrition is less an issue of solving starvation and more an issue of solving nutritional deficiencies. It's less an issue of enough calories and more an issue of the right calories. The majority of the U.S. population is above the starvation line. Some have argued that obesity has a disproportionate effect on Americans who are living closest to the poverty line. Clearly, their lack of income does not result in starvation—quite the opposite. These people are making choices about the food they eat, yet they are not making good choices. The "food aid is food eaten" assumption is not relevant to people who can elect to consume food that tastes better but is less nutritious.

The "Marketing Nutrition Is Like Marketing Soap" Perspective: Marketing Manager

A third perspective assumes that marketing nutrition to consumers is the same as marketing any other attribute of a product, whether it is fluoride for toothpaste, passenger side airbags for cars, or a spring fresh scent for a detergent. In reality, food is a very different venue than the more rational contexts of toothpaste and car shopping. For one, everyone is an expert with foods: We all know what we like. Yet the marketing of nutritious foods must delicately balance emotion with reason. Convincing someone to eat soy because it may help reduce weight will be unsuccessful if consumers sees it as a magic pill that will eliminate health problems or as something they have to tolerate—like medicine—before returning to a diet of hamburgers and fries.

The "Here Are the Results; My Work Is Done" Perspective: Researcher

A fourth perspective simply abdicates responsibility for the useful dissemination of relevant insights. The distracting multiple-project life of an active researcher can lead us to make a discovery and move on to the next project. Once the finding is published, we make far less effort to communicate and leverage it. Many papers take hundreds of hours to conceptualize, test, write, revise, and publish. In many fields it is common for projects to continue for six or more years before being published. If researchers and academics would allocate only 5 percent extra effort to helping disseminate or "market" the insights they generated, they could double their real-world impact.

Yet the notion of making a discovery more relevant, effective, or "marketable" is anathema to most academics (although that is the philosophy behind the founding of the land grant institutions that pay many of their salaries). Increasingly, however, the most effective academics are those who can conduct research while keeping an eye on how its results can best be implemented. In some cases this influences how or where the research is done; in other cases it can influence with whom it is done. This could be a partnership with a social scientist who focuses on the consumer adoption or it could be professionals who specialize in implementation. Simply being a biochemistry expert isn't enough anymore.

Not surprisingly, all four of these perspectives are common in the marketing of nutrition. Dietitians are well versed in the science behind the food, not in the acceptance of the foods. Government officials working with food aid often are experts in logistics and project management and are less familiar in consumer acceptance or compliance. Brand managers who find themselves working with "health foods" (perhaps as part of a two-year rotation) are experts in marketing, price promotions, and advertising for popular brands of soap and cereal. They are less familiar with a product that has little or no established following and that often necessitates a tradeoff between health benefits and the more easily promoted hedonic ones.

The objective of this book is to broaden and deepen the understanding of all four of these perspectives in a way that will help health professionals, government officials, brand managers, and researchers better encourage the adoption and consumption of nutritious foods among their constituents. For the dietitian, these people might be clients. For the government official, they might be people in disaster-stricken areas or developing countries. For the brand manager they may be people who are switching from less healthful brands to more healthful ones. For the researcher, they may be intermediary state extension experts or media representatives who are trying to make the findings relevant to the public.

Each of these perspectives brings its own set of biases. The fourteen chapters in *Marketing Nutrition* are intended to help each group gain a wider understanding of how to market nutrition and how to think about their specific situation. Each draws from original research that has been conducted in the Food and Brand Lab of the University of Illinois at Urbana-Champaign.

Organization of the Book

As shown in Figure I.2, the book is divided into five sections; each is briefly introduced here.

Part I: Secrets about Food and People

In this section, we will first look at the gap between what people know and what they do. This section examines the "nutritional knowledge is power" perspective because it shows that although nutritional knowledge is not necessarily related to good eating habits; certain combinations of nutritional knowledge are more likely to influence consumption than others. Chapter 1 demonstrates that whereas some people have no nutritional knowledge about a product such as soy, others know only about the attributes of soy and others know only about the health benefits of eating it. Interestingly, however, the findings in this chapter show that a

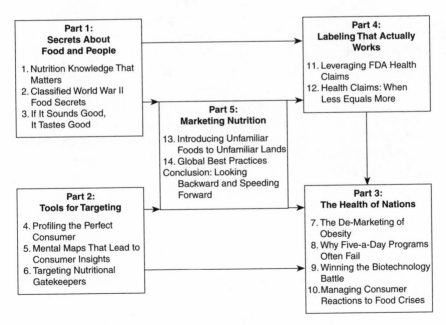

Part 1:
Secrets About
Food and People

1. Nutrition Knowledge That Matters
2. Classified World War II Food Secrets
3. If It Sounds Good, It Tastes Good

Part 2:
Tools for Targeting

4. Profiling the Perfect Consumer
5. Mental Maps That Lead to Consumer Insights
6. Targeting Nutritional Gatekeepers

Part 5:
Marketing Nutrition

13. Introducing Unfamiliar Foods to Unfamiliar Lands
14. Global Best Practices
Conclusion: Looking Backward and Speeding Forward

Part 4:
Labeling That Actually Works

11. Leveraging FDA Health Claims
12. Health Claims: When Less Equals More

Part 3:
The Health of Nations

7. The De-Marketing of Obesity
8. Why Five-a-Day Programs Often Fail
9. Winning the Biotechnology Battle
10. Managing Consumer Reactions to Food Crises

Figure I.2. Organization of *Marketing Nutrition*.

person is most likely to eat a healthful food when he or she knows about *both* the attributes of the food and how they lead to the health benefits of eating it.

Chapter 2 takes advantage of recently declassified Department of Defense studies that are relevant to our mission. Marketers often behave as though the problems they face are unique. Yet the marketing of nutrition has been problematic for many years. Many of today's problems of food acceptance are analogous to those faced during World War II, when the Committee on Food Habits tried to encourage Americans to eat organ meats to help address protein shortages caused by the war. Convincing people to eat organ meat in World War II was difficult: It was cursed with bad associations ("it's disgusting" and "it's not for people like me"), it wasn't part of a routine, and people didn't know how to prepare it. It is the same way with many healthful foods available today (such as soy). In chapter 2 we evaluate this previously ignored research to show that basic lessons about changing consumer tastes are as relevant today as they were during World War II.

People know what they like, right? Apparently not. Chapter 3 vividly illustrates that the tastes of consumers are very suggestible. Sometimes, simply changing the label of a package can cause them to notice ingredients that can dramatically bias their evaluation and their inclination to purchase the product. However, the effect of these labels varies across population segments. It is important to understand what can be done to communicate health information while minimizing taste aversion. This chapter also shows that descriptive names for foods make people taste what they believe they will taste. Descriptive names can influence a person's taste of a food, make the person believe the food has more calories, and even make the person believe that the restaurant at which they bought it is better. Although it is often said that there is no accounting for taste, we believe differently.

Part 2: Tools for Targeting

A good deal of the disconnection between nutrition education and behavior change can be attributed to ineffective targeting. Some people more easily comply with nutrition-related suggestions than others. Rather than approaching all people in a generic, one-size-fits-all manner, it is important to realize that some groups are more predisposed to some messages and interventions than others. Although the basic notion of segmenting and targeting consumers is not new, this section shows how tastes can be segmented and how nutrition education and marketing campaigns can become more efficient by taking these different tastes into account.

The first two chapters of this section examine techniques that can be used to identify the taste preferences and adoption likelihood among a number of market segments. Chapter 4 shows how to profile the ideal consumer. To best understand and target a person for nutritional change, it is effective to profile the person. Using soy as an illustration, this chapter shows how to profile ideal customers in a manner that enables better taste targeting.

Whereas chapter 4 examines the importance of using profiling as a method to better understand *who* the perfect consumers are, chapter 5 shows how mental mapping can be used to understand *why* they act (and eat) as they do. When trying to encourage people to eat a particular food, one can gain valuable insights by understanding why frequent consumers of the food like it so much. These perfect consumers have a mental map—associations and benefits—of the target food that helps explain why they like it so much. Identifying and illustrating these mental maps gives us insights into how we can convert infrequent consumers of the food into more frequent consumers.

A central theme of this section is that nutrition marketing efforts should be focused on the people who are most likely to be influenced or those who are most likely to influence others. Research consistently shows that good cooks are the nutritional gatekeepers of their homes, and they determine 72 percent of their family's food intake. Who are these good cooks, and how can they be categorized and targeted? Chapter 6 answers this question. Five general types of cooks make up more than 82 percent of the influential cooks in North America, but only three are likely to make selected nutritional foods a part of dinner on a regular basis.

Part 3: The Health of Nations

Part 3 addresses four of the more critical food-related issues facing developed countries today: decreasing obesity, increasing fruit and vegetable consumption, improving the understanding of biotechnology, and minimizing and managing food crises.

People want a variety of high-value, tasty foods that they can have in large quantities whenever convenient. This is one reason overeating at McDonald's is so much easier to do than convincing children to eat broccoli. Although they cater to our biological interests, food companies have recently been accused of contributing to the growing problem of obesity in the United States. After examining three inarguable consumer demands that led us to this problem, Chapter 7 outlines the five main drivers of food consumption and shows what smart marketers and motivated companies can and cannot do to counter the effect of each of these drivers in a "win-win" manner.

Chapter 8 begins by showing why Five-a-Day programs often fail in their objective of increasing fruit and vegetable consumption. These efforts are doomed from the start when they begin making generic appeals to all people. It is important to understand that taste profiles and behaviors of fruit lovers are different from those of vegetable lovers. Some people are more predisposed to one than another, and they should be targeted accordingly.

Although information can sometimes encourage a person to eat a food, in other cases it can prevent him or her from eating it. It's a risky business, and biotechnology is an important case in point. Chapter 9 shows that part of the reason why both proponents and opponents of biotechnology have been unsuccessful in changing the behavior of consumers is that they do not understand how consumers learn about biotechnology. One ongoing theme in this chapter is that the battle over nonorganic foods is never over. To maintain the trust and acceptance of a reasoned public, marketers must continuously address the health benefits and risks of biotechnology.

Yet even with continuous and open channels of communication, some segments of the public respond very differently to uncertainty and risk. The result can be public panic. Chapter 10 shows what happens when a food safety crisis threatens a food supply. Based on case studies and on data from the mad cow disease crises in Europe, generalizations can be made about how different people respond to different types of information. After describing these segments, suggestions are made on how to manage reactions through proactive precrisis preparations and crisis-related responses.

Part 4: Labeling That Actually Works

A general theme in this book is that different types of information influence different types of consumers in different ways. In this section, the question becomes how such information can be communicated in a way that has the most impact. To best leverage labels and nutritional claims, we focus specifically on how claims and labels can be made more compelling.

Communicating health benefits is especially important with Food and Drug Administration (FDA) health claims. It is often thought that the costly and time-consuming process involved in earning an FDA health claim will provide the magic key that increases a product's acceptance and solves all the marketing woes of producers and manufacturers. In most cases, however, the results of these claims are promising in the short run but disappointing in the long run. By looking at past successes and failures, chapter 11 shows how FDA claims have been best leveraged and how they can be better leveraged in the future.

With nutrition information, the message can be so confusing as to not have any impact on consumers. Chapter 12 examines how experimenting with different types of labels (long vs. short and front vs. back) can increase a label's persuasiveness. We provide evidence that combining a short label on the front of a package with a detailed label on the back of the package is the most persuasive way to communicate a health benefit.

Part 5: Marketing Nutrition

Whereas earlier chapters focused on profiling individuals and highly definable segments, chapter 13 shows how entire countries and cultures can be profiled to determine which will be the most likely to adopt various foods. An important question to food aid organizations and companies who have limited resources and distribution dollars is, "Which cultures will be most likely to adopt a given food most cost-effectively?" I develop a framework that shows how the food preparation methods and the strength of ethnic identity are key criteria in determining how quickly a country will adopt a new food. Case studies of Russia and Columbia show how this would be done in two different cultures. The basic framework that is developed can be used to help prioritize distribution efforts in any culture or segment. It can also be used to help estimate the effectiveness of various forms of food aid.

In chapter 14, I list a series of best practices from 153 functional food products across the world to provide tactical suggestions that have proven successful in helping incorporate functional foods into mainstream diets and long-term eating patterns. Five key themes are identified, and each is illustrated along with the specific best practices that relate to it. These best practices are categorized as relating to one of the four Ps of marketing: promotion, price, product, and place. These characteristics are known as the "marketing mix" because they represent four levers a marketer can use when trying to encourage a person to consider a particular product.

Although the boundaries between these characteristics are not always clear, this chapter provides a convenient way for a reader to begin organizing his or her marketing toolbox.

Conclusion

In the conclusion, I revisit the four commonly misleading perspectives described earlier. I then show how each chapter was intended to contribute to a change in perspective.

Summary

Throughout this book, a wide variety of products and contexts are used as illustrations. Beef might be the focus of one chapter and soy the focus of another, but they are all just examples to illustrate basic principles. They apply to other products and other contexts. The subtitle of this book—"Soy, Functional Foods, Biotechnology, and Obesity"—lists four important contexts and issues in which marketing nutrition has become important and visible. Although specific references are made to each throughout the book, the general principles often apply to all. Similarly, the renewed efforts to encourage the consumption of five fruits and vegetables a day can be made sharper, more focused, and more cost-effective based on the insights in this book. Although chapter 8 deals specifically with an approach to improve five-a-day programs, each chapter has ideas that can be appropriated and applied.

In the end, the true challenge in marketing nutrition is not in reinventing the wheel but in taking the lessons from the marketing failures and successes of others and applying them in other food-related contexts in a way that increases the chance of consumer acceptance. The same tools and insights that have helped make less nutritious products popular can also be used to bring people back to a healthful, more nutritious lifestyle.

PART ONE

Secrets about Food and People

ONE

Nutrition Knowledge That Matters

Many people want to believe that nutritional knowledge is power. That is, they believe that if we can simply educate people so that they can pass a nutrition quiz, they will all eat better.

Almost everyone knows that fruit is better for them than cookies, that a salad is better for them than french fries, and that broiled fish is better for them than a deep-fried pork chop. Despite this knowledge, cookie sales remain high, pork production is increasing, and even though a $0.99 garden salad at Burger King is less expensive than a $1.29 order of french fries, it is outsold by more than thirty to one.

Does nutritional knowledge really have such little impact on behavior? When past studies have tried to tie the two together, they typically compare people who have nutritional knowledge with people who have none. Yet "having knowledge" is not an all-or-nothing state. We have differing degrees of knowledge about almost everything. We have differing degrees of knowledge about the state capitals, about French nouns, and about nutrition. Few people know "all or nothing" about anything. The thesis of this chapter is that *how much* nutrition information consumers are given is less important than *what* information they are given.

Before examining what information we should try to communicate to consumers, it may be useful to see where consumers get the nutrition information they trust most. A 2002 study by the Food Marketing Institute found some insights relevant to the dissemination of nutrition information (Figure 1.1). The most frequently used and one of the most trusted

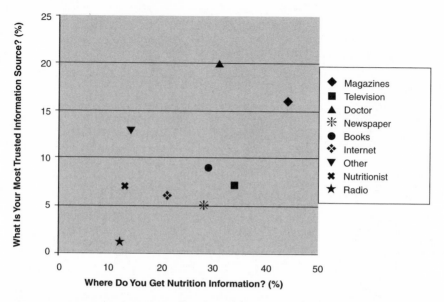

Figure 1.1. Where consumers get the nutritional information they trust. (Food Marketing Institute 2002.)

sources for nutrition education was magazines. Among the least used and least trusted sources were nutritionists.

Clearly something we are doing is wrong. We are not providing compelling, trusted information in an easily accessible manner. Perhaps we have been too concerned with the science and nuances of nutrition and not about the day-to-day, practical, low-involvement use of nutrition information. Let's examine the different types of nutrition information and how they appear to be used on a daily basis.

The Two Tiers of Nutritional Knowledge

Whether someone eats healthful foods is related partly to the type of knowledge he or she has about nutrition. The adoption of healthful foods is associated with two different tiers of knowledge. On a basic level, we can have attribute-level knowledge about a food. This is where we can identify a food's features or attributes, such as its calorie content, fat level, or protein density. On a higher level, we can have knowledge that is more consequence related. It is centered around knowing that "this food makes me fat" or "it is bad for my heart." Most nutrition education efforts are focused on attribute-level knowledge. It is focused on passing a multiple-choice nutrition quiz. This chapter focuses on how both types of knowledge are related to the acceptance and consumption of a functional food.

Throughout this book, *functional foods* refers to those that provide a health benefit beyond basic nutrition (Table 1.1). A functional food can be naturally functional (such as oatmeal, which contains cholesterol-reducing beta glucan), or it can contain an added ingredient that makes the traditional food functional (such as probiotic bacteria added to yogurt). Functional foods can be divided into categories based on whether they contribute to gut health (such as fermented yogurt drinks), bone health (such as calcium-enriched milk or juice), heart health (such as soy), or immune system health (such as broccoli). Functional foods can also be seen as embedded in a continuum ranging from normal foods (potatoes) to nutritious foods (fruit juice) to health foods (herbal tea) to functional foods (protein drinks) to medicine (vitamins).

With the recent increase in interest in diet and nutrition, encouraging people to eat functional foods has become faddish, and it has helped boost initial interest and sales. Unfortunately, people often are hesitant to try unfamiliar foods, even when they believe these foods to have healthful or functional properties. If people link their knowledge of a food's attributes to personal health-related consequences, they are more likely to accept and consume a new food. The relationship between food acceptance and

Table 1.1. Examples of Functional Foods and Potential Health Benefits

Functional Food	Key Component	Potential Health Benefits
Soy foods	Soy protein	Reduce cholesterol
Oats and oat-containing foods	Soluble fiber beta glucan	Reduce cholesterol
Black and green tea	Catechins	Reduce risk of cancer
Broccoli	Sulforaphane	Reduce risk of cancer
Tomatoes and tomato products	Lycopene	Reduce risk of cancer
Fruits and vegetables	Many different phytochemicals	Reduce risk of cancer and heart disease
Garlic	Sulfur compounds	Reduce risk of cancer and heart disease
Fish	Omega-3 fatty acids	Reduce risk of heart disease
Purple grape juice	Polyphenolic compounds	Support cardiovascular function
Yogurt and fermented dairy products	Probiotics	Improve gastrointestinal health

these different tiers of thinking is illustrated as a hierarchy of nutritional knowledge in Figure 1.2. This hierarchy of knowledge suggests that consumer knowledge about a food exists on multiple levels that range from attribute knowledge to consequence knowledge. Whereas attributes relate to the food, consequences relate to how the foods influence us (the consequences of consuming them).

People who have no knowledge of functional foods are unlikely to purchase them. Other people may have knowledge of a food's attributes, such as its calorie content or vitamin C level. Yet product attribute knowledge (on which much nutrition education has been focused) deals with only one portion of the knowledge hierarchy. Initial product knowledge involves understanding something about the food's attributes, but consumers are more likely to accept a functional food when they link their knowledge of that food's attributes to the personal consequences or benefits of consuming it. This is an important and useful insight. Linking food attribute knowledge to personal consumption consequence knowledge is more important than simply knowing a lot about a food's nutritional attributes or characteristics.

What Type of Nutritional Knowledge Influences Consumption?

Generally, functional foods are foods that provide a health benefit. They are foods or food components that can prevent disease or improve health

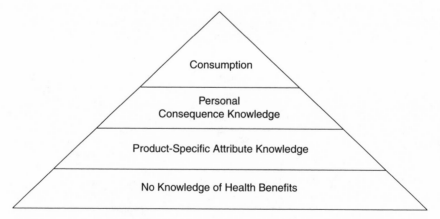

Figure 1.2. The hierarchy of functional food knowledge and consumption.

beyond what basic nutrients can do. They can consist of naturally fortified or enhanced foods and can produce advantageous health consequences or other desirable effects. Although many functional foods have been around for quite some time, their beneficial aspects continue to be discovered, and other foods are being engineered to contain such advantageous elements.

To better understand the relationship between these different types of knowledge and consumption behavior, we focus on soy. Its nutritional advantages and its perceived taste-related disadvantages make it both a promising and challenging illustration of how knowledge links to behavior.

To determine how a person's knowledge is connected to whether he or she eats nutritious foods, we developed a twelve-page survey that asked a number of questions regarding soy-related food preferences, soy-related knowledge, soy-related consumption, and functional food–related knowledge. The survey also asked people to write down anything they knew about functional foods and to write down everything they knew about soy. This was mailed to a random sample of 1,302 North Americans who were given a check for six dollars in exchange for completing the study. Approximately one-half of these people responded in a timely enough manner to be included in the study (61 percent female, average age 43 years; see Wansink and Chan 2001 for details).

People Have Little Knowledge of Functional Foods

Most people completing the survey were not familiar with the term *functional foods* (78 percent). Looking more specifically at soy, 39 percent of the respondents did not know of any health benefits it offered, and 4 percent thought it had no health benefits at all. Only 7 percent mentioned both attributes and consequences. Of those who mentioned attributes, 28 percent cited high protein content, and 24 percent noted a low fat content.

The most frequently mentioned consequences were that they believed it reduced the risk of cancer (5 percent), was nutritious (4 percent), was good for menopause and female diseases (4 percent), and helped reduce cholesterol levels (4 percent). Although 34.6 percent knew of product attributes, they did not necessarily link the properties of the product to self-relevant consequences.

Figure 1.3 shows the relationship between nutritional knowledge and the likelihood of knowingly consuming soy. People with no knowledge about the health benefits of soy consumed much less soy. Although hav-

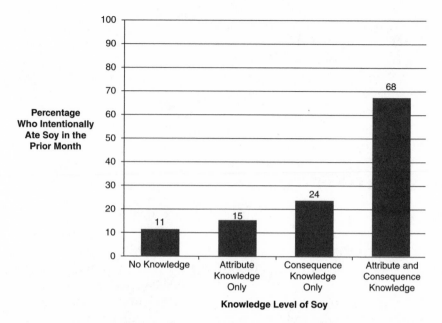

Figure 1.3. Having both attribute and consequence knowledge dramatically increases a consumers' willingness to eat a functional food.

ing either attribute-level knowledge or consequence-level knowledge increases the likelihood of consumption, it is not until those two characteristics are combined that consumption really takes off.

Linking Attribute with Consequence Knowledge Is Critical

One key finding here is that many people who knew the health attributes of soy did not understand the personal health consequences of consuming it. That is, they did not see a link between the attributes of the product and the personal health consequences of eating it. For instance, although many knew that soy has little fat content (24 percent) and cholesterol (11 percent), few knew that soy is good for weight control (0 percent) or for heart disease prevention (1 percent).

So why aren't people eating more soy? These results suggest that it's because they do not link product attributes of soy (such as low fat content and low cholesterol level) to self-relevant consequences (such as soy being good for weight control). This missing link may hinder the acceptance of functional foods such as soy and related products.

If We Know More, Will We Eat More?

Not necessarily. It is not how much we know but rather *what* we know that dictates whether we think we are eating nutritiously. Knowledge of a food's nutritional attributes or its consequences of consumption does not appear to relate strongly to one's consumption of that food; these types of knowledge increase consumption only when they are linked together. In this study, the 7 percent of people who link a food's attributes to personal positive consequences indicated a greater willingness to consume soy products than any other group. In particular, consumers who had only attribute-related knowledge, only consequence-related knowledge, or no knowledge at all, were all unlikely to buy soy products, buy soy-fortified meat, try soy dishes at restaurants, and buy microwaveable soy meals.

Although people might acknowledge the health benefits of a food, they are less likely to consume it if they don't link its attributes to the impact it will have on them. Many people know about the attributes of soy, a functional food, but they do not necessarily link that knowledge to self-relevant health consequences (nutritional benefits). Different types of knowledge about a food lead to different levels of consumption likelihood. Not all nutrition-related knowledge is equal. Such knowledge best translates into consumption when it links food attribute–related knowledge with consequence-related knowledge.

Linking knowledge of product attributes and personal consequences creates greater self-referencing, which results in greater likelihood of product acceptance. When consumers visualize themselves consuming a food—in their own food applications, ideas, and language—it confirms that the food is for them. People who link food attribute knowledge to personal consequence knowledge show a higher likelihood of consuming that food. Whether one looks at this information as a health care professional, a dietitian, a cook, or a consumer, it is clear that how much a person knows about functional foods is less important than what a person knows about them.

Lessons for Marketing Nutrition

This chapter reveals some basic but important insights about educating the public in order to change what they eat. Rather than overwhelming the public with health-related facts, concentrate on linking a few facts to personal attributes that consumers will be able to identify easily. In order to accept and adopt a functional food, consumers need to link the attributes of the product to the consequences of consuming it.

Applying consumer insights is important in marketing strategies for functional foods. The promotional aspect of marketing nutrition may be the most effective means of influencing consumers' attitudes. For example, when packaging functional foods, we need to realize that establishing a meaningful connection between product attributes and personal health consequences will stimulate more frequent usage. Promoting a product as low in cholesterol is less effective than saying it can help reduce the chances of heart disease. Often, the package itself is the first opportunity to teach the public about the health benefits of the product, and it also provides an opportunity to change consumers' behavior toward the food.

One of the key implications for practitioners is that educational strategies based on attribute knowledge of healthful products are not likely to change long-term behavior. Health care professionals and dietitians *must* link food attributes with personal health consequences when communicating with the public.

Marketing functional foods requires an understanding of how consumers make decisions. In chapter 2 I explore the processing styles of consumers and how they influence consumers' decisions.

For researchers, the hierarchy of knowledge illustrated in Figure 1.2 underscores the importance of differentiating between various types of knowledge when trying to understand consumers' knowledge-behavior link. It also suggests that a review of past research might show slightly different conclusions once we account for the types of knowledge that have been measured.

Related Readings

A more detailed version of this study and a more detailed discussion of the method used to assess the links between attributes and consequences are reported in the following articles:

Wansink, Brian, Randall E. Westgren, and Matthew M. Cheney (2005), "The Hierarchy of Nutritional Knowledge that Relates to the Consumption of a Functional Food," *Nutrition,* forthcoming.
Wansink, Brian, and Nina Chan. "Relation of Soy Consumption to Nutritional Knowledge," *Journal of Medicinal Foods* 4:3 (December 2001): 147–52.

TWO

Classified World War II Food Secrets

How can we get people to eat better? Many programs and campaigns to change eating habits, such as the "Five-a-Day" fruit and vegetable campaign, have met with costly, disappointing short-term results. Most recently, the adoption of healthful or functional foods has been slow because consumers are wary to try unfamiliar, initially unappealing foods such as soy. How can functional foods that appear unfamiliar or unappealing be incorporated into mainstream diets and long-term eating patterns? If we look back at World War II, we will find lessons that we can apply today to help address this question.

In the years just before and after America's involvement in World War II (1941–45), much domestic meat was being shipped overseas to feed soldiers and allies, causing concern that a lengthy war would leave the United States protein starved unless a protein substitute could be found. The potential solution to this shortage lay in what were then called variety meats or organ meats: hearts, kidneys, brains, stomachs, intestines, and even the feet, ears, and heads of cows, hogs, sheep, and chickens. The challenge was to encourage Depression-era Americans to incorporate them into their diets. To accomplish this, the Department of Defense enlisted Margaret Mead, Kurt Lewin, and dozens of the brightest and subsequently most famous psychologists, sociologists, anthropologists, food scientists, dietitians, and home economists to determine how dietary change could be accomplished.

Because World War II ended four years earlier than conservatively predicted, many of the recommendations from more than 200 of these studies were not implemented. Although dietary conditions are different today, some basic principles that motivated this classified research can be applied today as we seek to change lifestyles, food habits, and perceptions toward unfamiliar but nutritious foods.

In describing the context for this research, I provide an overview of the Committee on Food Habits and the philosophy of the two scholars behind it: Margaret Mead and Karl Lewin. I use the basic idea of reducing consumption barriers before providing consumption incentives to integrate selected studies conducted during the war. Finally, I discuss how these findings can be used to encourage lifestyle and diet changes.

World War II and the Committee on Food Habits

In the January 1943 edition of *What's New in Foods and Nutrition,* former President Herbert Hoover addressed the upcoming pressures related to food shortages.

> The homemaker controls the food consumption of the people. That problem will loom larger and larger in the United States as the war goes on. . . . Ships are too scarce to carry much of such supplies from the Southern Hemisphere; our farms are short of labor to care for livestock; and on top of it all we must furnish supplies to the British and Russians. Meats and fats are just as much munitions in this war as are tanks and aeroplanes. We should not wait for official rationing to begin to conserve. The same spirit in the household that we had in the last war can solve the problem. (Hoover 1943)

This proactive orientation made a strong distinction between restricted meats (traditional ones such as beef, pork, lamb, and sausage) and non-restricted meats, including liver sausage, liver, tongue, hearts, kidneys, sweetbreads, tripe, brains, pork feet, and ox tails. It also increased the need to facilitate large-scale changes in consumption behavior. Because the physical fitness of the entire population of the country was an important aspect of national security, the question arose as to what could be done to improve nutrition.

For this reason, the Committee on Food Habits (1940–47) was established by the National Research Council at the request of the Department of Defense. The purpose of the committee was to identify effective ways of adjusting the food habits of the American people. It was to accomplish this through a series of conferences and associated efforts to pool scientific knowledge for the benefit of the government agencies requesting their assistance and advice.

Because of the need for an integrating framework to understand this research, the highly visible anthropologist Margaret Mead was asked to serve as executive secretary for the Committee on Food Habits from 1942 to 1945. In this time period, it is estimated that more than 200 studies were directly or indirectly initiated, supported, or endorsed by the Committee on Food Habits. Through direct solicitations, interactions with colleagues, and calls for papers, Mead used six basic themes to organize what needed to be understood about food: the problem of food acceptability, food preparation and serving methods, sampling populations for food habit studies, problems in the feeding of military and civilian populations, regional and national habits and nutrition, and the relationship between food consumption habits and nutritional status. These themes were the focus of six conferences that helped generate insights on research methods and conceptual frameworks that could promote long-term changes in eating behavior.

It is largely recognized that, next to Mead's, the major contribution from the Committee on Food Habits was that of Kurt Lewin and his colleagues at the University of Iowa. After becoming a naturalized citizen in 1940, German-born Lewin was quickly given the required security clearance to consult on a wide spectrum of national problems because of his unique problem-solving approach. Lewin's basic premise (published posthumously as *Field Theory in Social Science* in 1951) was that all behaviors were determined by a balance of encouraging forces and discouraging forces (barriers and incentives). Whereas most efforts to change eating habits focused exclusively on increasing consumption incentives (eat nutritiously and be patriotic), Lewin believed the focus should be on systematically determining what barriers prevented someone from eating organ meats in the first place. By helping reduce the barriers that discouraged the consumption of organ meats, Lewin believed he could change the preparation and serving habits of the gatekeeping cook. This jointly held perspective of Mead and Lewin framed the research efforts of the Committee on Food Habits.

The Importance of Reducing Barriers to Consumption

Before 1942, the focus on changing eating habits reflected a stimulus-response model of propaganda and nutritional education. In contrast, Lewin and Mead believed that they first needed to reduce consumption barriers (decrease disincentives) before they could encourage people to change their eating habits. That is, before giving people nutritional or patriotic reasons why they should say "yes" to eating liver, it was important to first remove the reasons why they would say "no." Unless barriers to consumption were removed, promotional incentives would be wasted (Figure 2.1).

From the research sponsored by the Committee on Food Habits, four empirical themes emerge that suggest the fundamental characteristics of an accepted food. They can be summarized with the acronym SAFE. To be accepted, a food must be selected, available, familiar, and exactly as expected. In its most basic form, an acceptable food must taste good, be available, be familiar, and look, taste, and feel as expected. These empirical

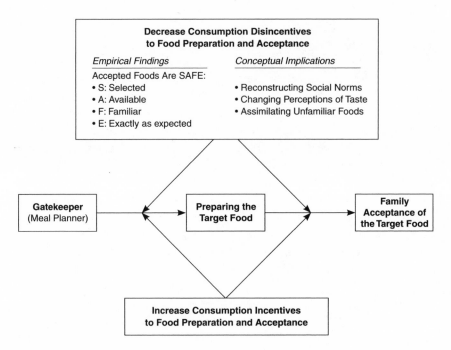

Figure 2.1. Gatekeeper-focused framework of food acceptance.

findings helped provide practical recommendations that were desired by the Committee on Food Habits. However, they also suggested that larger issues—social norms, perceptions of taste, and assimilation of variety—influenced human behavior. These three issues provide the organizing structure for the discussion on reducing barriers to food preparation and acceptance.

Reducing Barriers to Food Preparation and Acceptance

Gatekeepers control food through different channels (such as the garden, store, or pantry), and they play a central role in regulating consumption and dietary health. Yet it was typically believed that the "man of the house" determined what was eaten based on his preference for the food. Lewin's contrary view was that when food appeared on the table, it was often eaten despite a husband's preference. This was confirmed in a national survey that indicated that husbands and children often ate what was prepared for them and voiced strong opposition only when the meals became too novel or different. This insight provided a useful focus to the challenge of changing food habits. The effort to change food habits should *not* be broadly aimed at children or husbands. Instead, initial efforts should be aimed at the gatekeeper—the cook—who selects, purchases, prepares, and serves the food.

Interviews and observations of these gatekeepers indicated that key barriers to their buying and preparing organ meats centered around thinking it was not appropriate for them, thinking it would not taste good, and not knowing how to include it in meals (Radke and Klisurich 1947). These three barriers were addressed in research focusing on restructuring social norms, changing perceptions of taste, and increasing the assimilation of unfamiliar foods.

Restructuring Social Norms

One factor that inhibited organ meat consumption was that many people perceived organ meats as food that was not appropriate for someone like them to eat. Some perceived organ meats as useless parts of livestock to be discarded, and others perceived them as appropriate only for rural families or for lower socioeconomic groups.

People have distinct categories of food that they perceive as "food for us" and food that is appropriate for others (such as lutefisk or collards) or for animals (such as peanuts and cottage cheese for swine and corn for cattle). Kennedy (1945) found that a large number of now common food crops—carrots, lettuce, rye, wheat, and tomatoes—were widely introduced in California in the 1940s by the Mexicans, Chinese, and Armenians who lived there. Before then, most ethnic groups did not eat foods outside of their cultural food patterns unless they were repeatedly exposed to them across various occasions. In California, Mexicans were introduced to various leafy vegetables when they saw Chinese workers eat them as a staple in their diets. Consequently, leafy vegetables entered the Mexican diet in California and eventually led to a dramatic incorporation of these vegetables in their meals.

Although restructuring social norms is important in encouraging family acceptance at the dinner table, the strongest norm at the dinner table was found to be the example set by parents and friends. Families influence food habits and food acceptance to a great degree during childhood, and the social norms to eat organ meats were dramatically influenced by the mere presence of these foods on the family dinner table.

The power of parents in establishing social norms can be clearly seen in the South. People born and raised in the South are more likely to eat high-fat foods because many Southern families pass the tradition of deep-fried cooking from one generation to the next (Cummings 1945). Just as habits of regional cooking can be transferred through generations, the incorporation of organ meats into one's diet may have been part of a multigeneration process. Indeed, even though adult consumers were not particularly fond of organ meats, interviews and surveys indicated that they were more likely to incorporate organ meats into their diets as adults if they had been served them as children (Dickens 1945).

Foods also became more of a social norm when they were aligned with the patriotic obligation to do one's part for the war effort. They soon became foods that patriots ate, not necessarily foods that poor people ate. With this patriotic positioning, there was less of a fear of negative associations and dissonance. The war effort helped make organ meats more socially acceptable. Consuming organ meats was one way of showing support for the war effort on the home front. As a result, few people grumbled because to do so would be to minimize the greater sacrifices being made by others.

Changing Perceptions of Taste

One of the biggest barriers to consumer acceptance of organ meats was the perception that their taste was unacceptable. Recall the acronym

SAFE (Figure 2.1). Two factors that influenced a food's acceptability were whether it tasted good enough to be selected and whether it was served in a familiar form. Unfortunately, neither the flavor, appearance, nor texture of organ meats was familiar. Clearly, masking the taste with sauces, surrounding flavors, and side dishes was one solution, yet there were other drivers of taste that could be more directly influenced.

Familiar Preparation Influences Taste   Food preparation and serving methods can influence the acceptability of unfamiliar, even unpopular food items. Organ meats, especially liver entrées, were incorporated most successfully into wartime diets through similar preparation and serving methods as those of regular meats. Bollman's (1945) studies in this area were conducted with common, inexpensive vegetables, and it was found that the soldiers did not eat cabbage that was prepared differently from the ways in which they expected to see other vegetables prepared. Instead, soldiers were more likely to eat food, whether familiar or unfamiliar, when it was prepared in a way similar to their prior experiences and served in a familiar fashion. This was found to be consistent for both cooked vegetables and organ meats.

Familiar Appearance Influences Taste   Important work regarding preservatives indicated that making organ meats look familiar (through their cuts, shapes, and packaging) influenced perceptions of taste. This insight was found during research on what made preserved foods most acceptable. At the beginning of World War II, there was a need for canned meats that tasted like fresh meat, for powdered milk that was reconstituted to taste like fresh whole milk, and for preserved bread that tasted like fresh bread. The government pushed food companies to preserve foods to resemble fresh foods. Because they looked and tasted fresh, people believed they must be safe and that preservatives were not harmful (Patten 1998).

Because of this work, initial efforts introduced some organ meats as filler in ground beef and sausages. In both ground meat and sausage forms, replacing existing meat with organ meats was accepted because they did not cause the meat to look differently than expected.

Taste Portfolios Influence Taste   Given that one way to introduce unfamiliar foods is to combine them with existing foods, an important question is what dominates one's evaluation or assessment of a full-plate meal. Do unfamiliar foods drive these evaluations, or do familiar, favorable foods do so?

To answer this, Polemis altered the favorability (favorable vs. unfavorable) and the form (main dish vs. side dish) of various hot lunches in Iowa high schools in 1943. Her studies show that high favorability for a main dish caused less variation in the evaluation of the meal (regardless of the favorability of the side dishes). However, favorability of the main dish makes side dishes very important in evaluating the meal. The implications for organ meats would be to prepare highly palatable main dishes while incorporating organ meats into the side dishes until organ meats became more preferred and widely accepted.

Though related to taste, these studies related to how subjective beliefs and perceptions—not objective reality—influence attitudes and behavior. In their studies at the University of Illinois, Fishbein and Ajzen (1975) used examples from this context to show that subjective beliefs influenced attitudes. They extended this finding to show that these attitudes are combined with social norms to determine whether a person will eat a new food such as an organ meat.

Assimilating Unfamiliar Foods

As the availability of restricted meat (beef, pork, and lamb) decreased at the butcher shop, the availability of organ meats increased. This increased availability stimulated perceptions of organ meat acceptability and increased gatekeepers' willingness to experiment with these meats. When first learning how to prepare organ meats, gatekeepers were encouraged to prepare and serve them in the manner consistent with typical expectations for meat. One of the best ways to present this food was to position it in combination with familiar foods and to prepare them in a manner similar to how favored meats were prepared. Consider the following excerpt from a 1943 article called "Share the Meat," in *What's New in Foods and Nutrition:* "There are so many ways to serve variety meats, along or in combination with other foods, that they will be a boon in supplementing the rationed meats. Every husband will cheer for steak and kidney pie. Liver may be a problem with the children which can be solved by liver loaf—and so may the lunch-box meal. Backed stuffed hearts are as attractive as they are appetizing. Brains and sweetbreads delight the epicure. Ox tail soup satisfies hearty appetites" (Wilson 1943, p. 38).

Early programs for integrating alternative protein sources were nearly always focused on only one type of organ meat. These "all or nothing" programs neglected to incorporate variety, and they led to very low levels of adoption. Bollman (1945) was commissioned to study unfamiliar food acceptance by investigating the role of variety.

High Levels of Variety Help Increase Food Acceptance Using pork roast in several Army mess halls, Bollman (1945) discovered that the pork roast became objectionable when it was served too often, even when different preparation methods were alternated. Yet when a variety of other foods were served throughout the week, pork roast was rated as much more favorable. To further investigate the need for variety, Mead (1945) looked into flexible adjustment programs: programs that consist of a variety of food alternatives. She found that programs offering variety were more successful in achieving long-term change than programs that offered less variety. Organ meats were promoted by increasing the variety of available meat options, thereby preventing monotony.

The important insight was that gradually introducing unfamiliar foods in to one's diet helped make the foods more acceptable because they were then viewed as something novel and not as long-term or permanent substitutes. Introducing a rotation of variety meats into occasional meals (instead of into every meal) was the most successful approach because of the gradual acclamation it allowed.

Gradually Introducing Unfamiliar Food Can Lead to Greater Acceptance Although this research focused on food, it had an unexpected impact on the development of social judgment theory, specifically assimilation-contrast theory. Whereas people refused to make dramatic changes in their dietary patterns—such as eating organ meats multiple times each week—they were more amenable to eating them in a less frequent manner that contrasted less with their existing eating patterns. Insisting on all-or-nothing adoption of a new behavior or belief was found to be less effective than encouraging one that was more moderate.

Increasing the Incentives to Consume

Whereas a focus on reducing consumption barriers characterized the majority of the research during the war, attention was also given to increasing the incentives to consume organ meats. Early efforts in this area were directed at understanding the motivation behind food consumption. The key concern was that nutritional knowledge does not dictate behavior.

Consistent with what was presented in chapter 1, knowing that a food is nutritionally beneficial did not often lead to long-term adoption.

To better understand this link between nutritional knowledge and behavior, Mead (1943) proposed a campaign that asked consumers to be responsible and intelligent in using science to increase their ability to function in society. Because people were already supportive of war efforts, they were predisposed toward seeing how scientific findings could enhance their welfare. They then perceived the resulting change in their behavior as being voluntary rather than forced.

When focusing on how to better educate and persuade gatekeepers, the most notable studies compared discussions with lectures. In the initial study that sparked many others throughout the war, Lewin investigated two methods of learning by offering various groups of Iowa mothers pediatric information about the nutritional merits of incorporating an unusual additive into their infant formula (1943). Some of these groups were informed using a discussion-decision method, whereas others were informed using a lecture method. It was found that the groups informed by the discussion-decision method were three times more likely to consider and adopt infant formula containing the additive. Given the success of this study, Lewin (1951) then examined these two educational methods in the context of organ meat adoption, where the discussion-decision method tended to generate nearly five times the level of trial as the lecture method.

Although much of this research focused on gatekeepers, Radke and Caso (1948) showed that it could also be used on a broader level. They tested the effectiveness of the two educational methods among 850 children from Weeks Junior High School in Newton, Massachusetts. Although both methods were initially successful in encouraging children to choose nutritionally adequate lunches, only the discussion-decision method generated lasting results. It was concluded that this method encourages longer-term change because it involves active behavior and public commitment rather than the passive decisions made by the lecture group. Passive decisions have less emphasis on the behavioral reinforcements that bring about long-term change.

The long-term acceptance of organ meats was facilitated when people who made a personal commitment to eat organ meats were publicly and socially reinforced for their behavior. The government publicly reinforced organ meat consumption through rationing and advertising messages, and societal reinforcement was achieved through organ meat availability at the butcher shop and support for the war effort.

Lessons for Marketing Nutrition

The work of the Committee on Food Habits emphasized the importance of removing barriers to consumption before trying to change food habits. Since then, however, many researchers and marketers have ignored this approach and returned to incentive-oriented persuasion. For instance, many efforts in nutrition education focus on increasing awareness and comparing the effectiveness of different message strategies. Yet any efforts to increase consumption incentives will be compromised if not preceded by efforts to reduce consumption barriers.

Human behavior regarding consumption is influenced by social norms, perceptions of taste, and variety. This has important implications for dietitians, brand managers, developmental scientists, and opinion leaders. For instance, if we want to help consumers replace less nutritious foods with more nutritious foods, we need to realize that external factors such as food preparation or serving methods can influence the acceptability of unfamiliar or unpopular food items. These organ meat studies of World War II give us an insight into how we can get people to eat healthful foods. First we need to help them make it part of their routine and show them how to prepare it. In particular, to be widely accepted, foods must be selected, available, familiar, and expected (SAFE).

From the lessons learned in the chapter, we can conclude that we should position a marketed functional food in combination with familiar foods and prepare it in a similar manner as favored foods. We may also want to associate the food with an important value held by the consumer. During the war, people ate organ meats to support the soldiers; perhaps we can use this same notion with current functional foods so that people eat more fruits and vegetables.

A change in consumer eating behavior is most easily accepted when the change is gradual. For nutrition marketing, we learn from the studies discussed in this chapter that if we wanted to increase the consumption of soy, for example, we should aim to replace just a few meals a week with soy and gradually increase soy consumption over time. This way, we develop a routine for consumers to follow, and consumer behavior is more easily changed. Introducing foods gradually into one's diet helps make them more acceptable because they become viewed as something novel and not as long-term or permanent substitutes. In chapter 3, we will look at how culture can either facilitate or can side-track food consumption decisions.

Consider the problem of weight control and the concern that the long-term maintenance of dietary regimens may be as low as 20 percent. Some of the basic insights from sixty years ago—restructuring social norms, changing perceptions of taste, and assimilating unfamiliar foods—can be used today by institutions, public policy officials, companies, and individuals to reduce the structural and psychological barriers that interfere with weight control. For instance, insights on how to assimilate unfamiliar foods would be useful to health professionals or marketers of nutritious, functional foods who want to help consumers replace less nutritious foods with more nutritious foods. Assuming the healthful food is widely available, this could include substituting high-fat foods with low-fat foods, substituting sweet snacks with fruit, substituting starches with vegetables, or substituting meat protein with soy protein.

For healthful products, the goals would be to make them seem more similar to the product to be replaced on dimensions such as palatability, texture, and flavor. The taste of low-fat products can be improved by making their appearance and taste match those of favored products. Along those same lines, taste and packaging can create a sense of familiarity. For example, the brand Tofutti includes a wide range of soy-based frozen desserts that look and taste like traditional frozen desserts. In this instance, consumers see soy ice cream as an acceptable substitute for ice cream because it has a similar appearance, texture, and package.

Related Reading

Further detail about these recently declassified World War II studies from the Committee on Food Habits can be found in the following article, from which this chapter has been adopted:

Wansink, Brian. "Changing Eating Habits on the Home Front: Lost Lessons from World War II Research," *Journal of Public Policy and Marketing* 21:1 (Spring 2002): 90–99.

THREE

If It Sounds Good, It Tastes Good

To what extent do labels influence our taste of a product? Can a label actually make us think a food tastes good or bad? Although this general issue of taste suggestibility is not often academically studied, it has a rich anecdotal history. Studies during World War II examined the feasibility of serving organ meats (such as brains, kidneys, tongue, and liver) as potential replacements for shortages of more traditional meats. Whereas initial taste was nearly acceptable when organ meats were unlabeled, once they were labeled, the taste was rated as unequivocally unacceptable by many segments of people (Wansink 2002). Therefore, when thinking about marketing nutrition, it is important to evaluate how powerful a label can be in influencing taste.

This raises two issues: do healthful ingredient names make foods taste worse, and do evocatively descriptive names make foods taste better? If labels influence how we think a food tastes, perhaps dietitians, marketers, and even mothers can change the taste of a food by simply changing its name. In any case, there is little "literature on how advertising, packaging, and information generate sensory expectations" (Deliza and MacFie 1996) and less still on how they translate into postconsumption taste ratings.

The wrong word may cause people to dislike the taste of a product. Consider a healthful product such as soybeans. Although many people know soybeans are nutritious, many also tend to dislike their taste. As with organ meats in the 1940s, it may be that even the suggestion that a food contains this healthful ingredient may be so powerful that it may cause people to dislike a product that they believe might contain soy (regardless of whether it does).

In contrast, using the right combination of words may help make a product taste better. That is, whereas the word *soy* may negatively influence the taste of a food, descriptive labels such as *homestyle* or *country classic* may improve the taste of a food. The use of descriptive labels is an emerging trend in the hospitality industry (such as Jack Daniels® Chicken, Psychedelic Sorbet®, or the Booming Onion®), but does simply changing the menu labels from generic, straightforward names to descriptive names affect sales or make a customer believe the food tastes better?

This chapter examines the extent to which our taste resides in our head as well as on our tongue. After providing some background about this notion, I describe studies that show how names influence our taste.

Suggesting a Taste: Why Names Influence Our Taste

One's prior expectations of a food can influence subsequent posttaste evaluations. Yet like perceptions of quality, these evaluations can be subtly influenced. Even information related to a food's fat content, for instance, has been shown to influence taste expectations and taste ratings (Kahkonen and Tuorila 1998).

When in restaurants, people scan menus looking for items they believe will satisfy their expectations. Consider how people evaluate "Grandma's homemade chocolate pudding." If they perceive Grandma's cooking as being flavorful, they may combine their beliefs about the characteristics of Grandma's cooking (flavorful) with the characteristics of chocolate pudding (sweet and smooth). These expectations can establish an affect state (Mela 1999) that can bias their evaluation of its taste. Unless these expectations are dramatically disconfirmed, their taste ratings generally appear to be consistent with prior expectations (Cardello 1994).

As long as the foods are not too different (worse) than what was expected, these favored associations appear to form an attitude halo. Given an evocative descriptive food label, one's evaluations are more likely to reflect thoughts in a similar direction.

In contrast, however, if a label contains a description or an ingredient that is not perceived as favorably tasting, their preconceptions could negatively bias their taste. Research has found that people who have not acquired a taste for soy have negative perceptions of the taste, aftertaste, and texture of soy products. My colleagues and I investigated whether the expectation that a product contains soy would bias posttaste evaluations of the product. If the mere thought that a product contains a particular ingredient can bias one's taste, such a product will have difficulty gaining acceptance. To test this notion, we examined a product that contains no soy.

The Phantom Ingredient Taste Test

To better examine the effect of ingredient labeling, Se-Bum Park and I designed a blinded taste test and recruited 148 adults to participate. Each person was given a nutrition bar that was labeled as containing "10 grams of soy protein" or one that was labeled as containing "10 grams of protein" (there was no mention of soy). All participants were given the same nutrition bar; only the labeling was different, and neither bar contained soy protein. We call this a phantom ingredient blinded test because the ingredient purported to be contained in some of the bars was absent. Through this method, we could measure "pure" effects of the soy label on peoples' expectations and perceptions. Consumers were asked to try the nutrition bar and to answer a series of open-ended questions. Then they were asked to evaluate the product's taste, nutrition, and fat content, and their food attitude, purchase intention, and past usage behavior on a nine-point scale.

What a Difference a Label Makes

People who tried the nutrition bar that made no mention of soy generally liked the taste and texture of the bar and made favorable comments about the product. In contrast, those who ate the nutrition bar that was labeled as containing soy made more negative comments about it. They were more likely to complain of an unpleasant taste (37 percent vs. 10 percent), and they were more likely to comment about the product having an unpleasant aftertaste (18 percent vs. 3 percent). Because there was no soy in the product, it appears that the soy label biased participants' perception of the product.

In addition to evaluating participants' open-ended comments, we evaluated their taste ratings (Figure 3.1). People who believed they were consuming a soy-based food rated it as having a poor taste and a poor

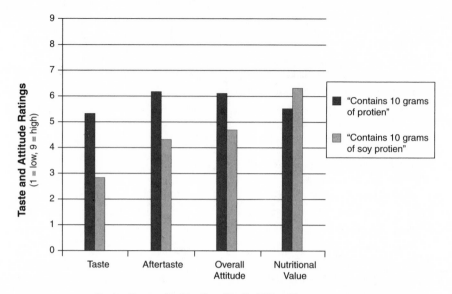

Evaluations after Tasting the Nutrition Bar

Figure 3.1. Soy labels' effects on taste evaluations and perceptions of nutritional value.

aftertaste. Although they had a more favorable perception of its healthfulness, they still had an unfavorable attitude toward it. In this case the perceived taste of a food drove food attitudes more than perceptions of its healthfulness.

How Does Labeling Influence Health-Conscious Consumers?

These results raise other questions, such as whether someone who is health oriented will be favorably influenced by the inclusion of a healthful ingredient on a label. To address this question, we designed a second experiment in which a soy label ("contains 10 grams of soy protein" vs. "contains 10 grams of protein") was crossed with a health claim ("May help reduce the risk of heart disease" vs. no health claim), and a general population (the taste-conscious segment) was given the nutrition bars along with a group that was identified as a health-conscious segment. In a study similar to the one just described, 155 adults were randomly given a nutrition bar in a realistic wrapper that had one of the four different labels (soy label vs. no soy label; health claim vs. no health claim) on it. After tasting the product, which contained no soy, they were asked to write down their thoughts and feelings about the product. Then they were asked about their taste perceptions, attitudes, and purchase likelihood.

Participants in the taste-conscious segment who ate the bars labeled as containing soy rated them as tasting and looking worse than those in the nonsoy condition; those in the health-conscious segment were uninfluenced by the soy label. That is, having soy on the product did not hurt their taste evaluation, but it also did not help. These results confirm that the taste perceptions of taste-conscious consumers are more sensitive to soy labeling than those of health-conscious consumers.

In both groups, however, combining the soy label with the health claims increased the believability of the claims. In contrast, when bars were labeled with a health claim but there was no mention of soy, people did not believe the claim. These results may provide a starting point to marketers who want to develop market segmentation strategies for soy-based packaged foods. They show that soy claims can be beneficial to targeted market segments when associated with a health claim.

Can Descriptive Names Improve Taste Perceptions?

The two studies just described show how labels can negatively bias one's perceived taste of a food. They show that if a person believes a product contains an ingredient thought to taste bad, it negatively influences their taste ratings and overall evaluation. What the studies do not show is whether the reverse is true. That is, if we descriptively label a food in a favorable way, will it cause people to think the food tastes better?

Descriptive names might add a positive halo to a food, or they might unfairly raise expectations that lead to disappointment. Research on labeling has focused on nutritional labels, health labels, and warning labels, but much less has been directed toward descriptions or names on labels. Descriptive names might add a positive halo to a food, they might have little effect, or they might backfire if they unfairly raise expectations that lead to disappointment. Jim Painter, Koert van Ittersum, and I examined this question in a more realistic environment by moving the study to a cafeteria to see how the use of descriptive names for six different foods would influence sales and intended repatronage of the restaurant.

The Cafeteria Study

To determine how people respond to descriptive labels, we conducted a six-week field experiment in a cafeteria at the University of Illinois. After reviewing the past sales of products in the cafeteria, we selected six products that were popular enough to offer twice a week and that represented a wide variety of foods. Descriptive labels included a wide mix of geographic labels, nostalgia labels, and sensory labels that were presented on menu boards and next to the items in the cafeteria line. The foods were given the following names:

Regular Menu Item Names	Descriptive Menu Item Names
Red beans with rice	Traditional Cajun red beans with rice
Seafood filet	Succulent Italian seafood filet
Grilled chicken	Tender grilled chicken
Chicken parmesan	Home-style chicken parmesan
Chocolate pudding	Satin chocolate pudding
Zucchini cookies	Grandma's zucchini cookies

During the Tuesday and Friday lunch of each of the six test weeks, two of the items were presented with a regular or basic label (e.g., "grilled chicken"), two items were presented with a descriptive label, and two items were not offered. For the next two weeks, the items and the conditions were systematically rotated until all menu items were present in all conditions. In the fourth week, the rotation was repeated. During a six-week period, each item was available six times. Everyone who selected one of the six target menu items from the cafeteria line was asked to complete a questionnaire by the person at the cash register. Each of the 140 diners was asked single-item questions related to product appearance, taste, and calorie content and how full they felt.

Descriptive Labels Make Boring Foods Better

Do descriptive labels influence taste perceptions? Definitely. Descriptive labels increased sales by 27 percent (see Wansink, Painter, and van Ittersum 2001) and caused diners to rate these foods as more appealing, tastier, and higher in calories. These labels also influenced perceptions of the quality and value of the foods (Figure 3.2). Descriptive labels influenced nearly every aspect of the eating experience.

The sensory-related benefits of labeling had a referred impact on the

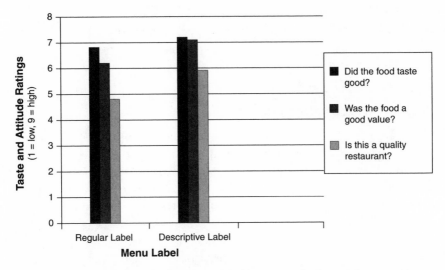

Figure 3.2. Descriptive labels favorably influence tastes and attitudes.

restaurant itself. When a person ate a descriptively labeled food, he or she was more likely to think the restaurant was up to speed with food trends and that it was a high-quality establishment. Such labels also influenced how soon participants said they would return to the restaurant.

Why do labels have such a dramatic impact? Part of what descriptive labeling allows consumers to do is to concentrate more on their feelings and on the taste of the foods. When asked to comment on their entrée or dessert, people who were given a descriptively labeled product focused 84 percent of their comments on factors related to the taste and sensory nature of the product. In contrast, those who ate the less descriptively labeled products focused only 42 percent on these sensory aspects and reserved their remaining comments for the more utilitarian or functional characteristics of the foods, such as it being "filling" or "reasonably priced."

The name of a food is an important decision-making criterion. When the foods with descriptive names were of high quality, participants considered them more appealing, tasty, and satisfying and believed they were higher in calories. Those who saw the descriptively named products were much more likely to focus on the positive aspects of the foods than the negative aspects.

Providing descriptive labels not only enhances the perceived attractiveness of menu items but also may improve the consumption experience. Descriptive labels such as "Grandma's zucchini cookies" increased sales by 27 percent, improved posttrial evaluations of quality and value, improved attitudes toward the restaurant, and increased participants' likelihood of returning to the restaurant.

Generating Descriptive Names

There are a number of different ways to generate descriptive labels, including the use of geographic labels ("Cajun" or "Italian"), nostalgia labels ("homestyle" or "Grandma's"), or sensory labels ("tender" or "satin"). The type of label that would be most effective depends on the product it describes. Certain types of labels work better with certain foods than others.

As we note in the *Cornell Hotel and Restaurant Administration Quarterly,* one method used to generate descriptive names is to brainstorm food-related associations that can tie the food to relevant places, memories, or descriptive adjectives. A second method is to note the variety of descriptive names used at different restaurants, such as high-end restaurants and theme restaurants. These can stimulate one's thinking about food names relevant to their situation. In general, it is important to realize that customers associate the descriptions on labels with their expectations of how the food will taste and make them feel. Vivid adjectives that portray geographic, nostalgic, or sensory themes can help trigger these anticipated feelings and expectations. Here are some suggestions that owners and managers in the hospitality industry can use to generate some of these themes.

Geographic Labels   Labels that claim to reproduce the same flavors that are specifically found in geographic areas have proven successful. The key is in deciding which region is appropriate for the product and then deciding which adjectives create that image or ideology (e.g., "southwestern Tex-Mex salad," "London fish and chips," "real Carolina barbecue," or "country peach tart").

Nostalgia Labels   Alluding to past time periods can trigger happy memories of family, tradition, and nationalism. Customers sometimes like the feeling of eating something wholesome and traditional (e.g., "classic old-world Italian," "legendary chocolate mousse pie," "ye olde potato bread," or "Nana's favorite chicken soup").

Sensory Labels If labels accurately describe the taste, smell, and mouth feel of the menu item, then customers can more easily picture themselves eating it. Although ice cream shops accomplish this masterfully, with names such as "chocolate velvet," sensory labels can also be found on other creative menus (e.g., "hearty, wholesome steaks," "snappy seasonal carrots," or "buttery, plump pasta").

Brand Labels Another category of labels involves a cross-promotion with a related brand that has important associations that make the menu item more attractive. The idea of cross-promotions is not new, but it is catching on in the chain and franchise restaurant world. One drawback of brand labels is that the legal costs and licensing costs can be too expensive for single restaurants. The use of brands says to consumers, "If you love the brand, you'll love this menu item" (e.g., "Black Angus® beef burgers," "Jack Daniels® BBQ ribs," or "Butterfinger® blizzard").

One way to generate ideas for descriptive labels is to sit down with a pencil and think of food-related associations that tie in to relevant places, memories, or descriptive adjectives. A second way to jump-start your descriptive labeling talent is to take a pencil and paper and write down the variety of descriptive labels used at different restaurants. Two great places to start are theme restaurants and ice cream stores.

Lessons for Marketing Nutrition

When blind taste tests raise the awareness of ingredients or attributes, they can artificially inflate or deflate sensory ratings, evaluations, and food attitudes. Dietitians in institutional or private settings may be able to improve perceptions of a food's appearance and taste by giving it a favorably descriptive name. This may be particularly valuable when one is trying to facilitate the introduction of unfamiliar foods. For instance, recent studies have investigated how different names (such as "soya") can improve people's perceptions of products containing soy.

Overcoming the Taste Stigma of "Health Foods"

This chapter presents three important insights about how a healthful ingredient label influences the product preference and perception of different segments of consumers. First, taste is subjective. People will taste what they expect to taste, and it is important not to negatively bias expectations. When encouraging consumption of an unfamiliar but healthful ingredient (such as soy), it is important to realize that mentioning the ingredient on a label may negatively influence a person's taste perception and may even prevent the person from eating the food in the future.

Yet although soy labels generated some negative perceptions, they helped decrease consumers' skepticism toward health- or energy-related claims. Soy labels negatively influenced taste perceptions, they positively influenced perceptions of nutrition. Therefore, using healthful ingredient labels and health claims together may neutralize negative perceptions that might result from using either alone.

A second insight from these findings is that consumers are not equally influenced by suggestive labeling. It may be that some people are more suggestible than others. We generally find that a large percentage of consumers taste what they want to taste. However, the taste-conscious consumer segment is the segment most negatively influenced by soy labeling. Marketers can emphasize other ingredients that override the negative perceptions of soy. Evocative packaging, logos, and brand name characters have helped ease the acceptance of products, partly because they reduce counterarguing. Similarly, product and situation comparisons help distract consumers from the negative perceptions they might have of soy. In addition, marketers can emphasize health-related claims more strongly than they emphasize soy as an ingredient, or they can find host products that override the perceived taste of soy.

It is important to realize that ingredient labeling can favorably influence certain segments of consumers (health oriented vs. taste oriented). For other segments, however, labeling a menu item or institutional food might be more effective when it describes the flavor (such as "whole-grain vegetarian burgers") instead of the ingredient ("soy burgers").

A third insight from these findings points to recent work that has begun to differentiate the types of profiles of consumers who prefer soy-related products for their taste (taste-motivated consumers) from consumers who prefer soy-related products more for their health benefits (health-motivated consumers). Two different studies involving consumers from North America and from India have shown consistent results. People who consume soy foods primarily for their taste are more likely to claim they live with great cooks and appreciate fine food, and they also tend to be adventurous opinion leaders and wine drinkers. Although both taste-motivated and health-motivated people tend to be more favorably predisposed to a soy-labeled product than nonconsumers of soy, we may find that soy labeling has differing sensory influences on the two segments because of the more fundamental differences in their personalities and in how they view food. Such key segmentation distinctions can be further considered in decisions related to the production, labeling, and marketing of soy-related foods.

People who deal with a specific ingredient (such as scientists, engineers, marketers, or health advocates) often lose sight as to how the ingredient is perceived outside their circle of like-minded advocates. Although many of those who work closely with soy might enthusiastically believe that a soy label is advantageous, it does not seem as though the general population agrees.

Using Descriptive Names to Make Foods Taste Better

Whereas the wrong words can unfavorably bias a person's taste ratings of a product, the right words can favorably bias them. Providing descriptive names not only enhances the perceived attractiveness of menu items but also may favorably influence the actual consumption experience. Stated differently, simple descriptive labels such as "Grandma's zucchini cookies" increased sales by 27 percent, improved posttrial evaluations of quality and value, improved restaurant-related attitudes, and increased restaurant repatronage intentions.

Clearly the suggestive power of labeling has some immediate applications for helping increase the acceptance and consumption of nutritious foods. Consider the following:

- Dietitians in institutional or private settings can improve perceptions of a food's appearance and taste by providing them with descriptive labels.
- The use of descriptive menu labels may facilitate the introduction of unfamiliar functional foods.
- Descriptive menu labeling can take the form of geographic labels, nostalgic labels, and sensory labels.
- Foods that are descriptively labeled should be of above-average quality in order to minimize backlash from unmet expectations. Using an unmerited descriptive label might backfire and negatively influence customers' attitudes about the item.

Customers associate descriptive names with their expectations of how the food will taste and make them feel. Vivid adjectives that portray geographic, nostalgic, or sensory themes can help trigger these anticipated feelings and expectations. For instance, geographic names that claim to reproduce the same flavors that are found in those geographic areas are successful if adjectives are used to create that image or ideology. Similarly, nostalgia names alluding to past time periods can trigger happy memories of family, tradition, and identity. In the cafeteria study, the descriptive names that were used had been pretested to evoke favorable associations with the food, and all the food used in this study was of reasonably high quality. If the food was of only average or below-average quality, descriptive names may have had less of an impact. Indeed, using an unmerited descriptive label might backfire and negatively influence customers' attitudes about the item.

An interesting question is whether descriptive names lead people to consume more of the food than they otherwise would. If descriptive names improve a person's sensory perceptions of the food, they might also influence how much the person wants to eat. Conversely, if descriptive names also lead people to believe the food is higher in calories (as we found), they may decrease how much the person eats.

Further Readings

This chapter is drawn from a series of studies conducted at the University of Illinois. Details of the methods and of more extensive findings can be found in the following articles:

Wansink, Brian. "Overcoming the Taste Stigma of Soy," *Journal of Food Science* (September 2003b).

Wansink, Brian, James M. Painter, and Koert van Ittersum. "Descriptive Menu Labels' Effect on Sales," *Cornell Hotel and Restaurant Administration Quarterly* 42:6 (December 2001): 68–72.

Wansink, Brian, Koert van Ittersum, and James E. Painter. "How Descriptive Food Names Bias Sensory Perceptions in Restaurants," *Food Quality and Preference,* forthcoming.

Wansink, Brian, and Se-Bum Park. "Sensory Suggestiveness and Labeling: Do Soy Labels Bias Taste?" *Journal of Sensory Studies* 17:5 (November 2002): 483–91.

Wansink, Brian, Se-Bum Park, Steven Sonka, and Michelle Morganosky. "How Soy Labeling Influences Preference and Taste," *International Food and Agribusiness Management Review* 3 (2000): 85–94.

PART TWO

Tools for Targeting

FOUR

Profiling the Perfect Consumer

At least some part of the population will adopt an unfamiliar but nutritious food simply because it's more healthful, but a larger portion will do so only if the taste of this food is preferable to alternatives. To better understand the types of people who have adopted a healthful unfamiliar food, it could be beneficial to profile those who did so because they like the taste.

In contrast to health-motivated food choices ("I eat it because it's supposed to be good for me"), taste-motivated preferences have long been shown to provide an enduring motivation for dietary change. Why should we care why someone eats a food as long as he or she eats it? One concern with a health-motivated segment for any product is that their behavior often is seen as more fickle than that of those who consume a product for more hedonic reasons such as taste. When the health risk is no longer a salient concern or when there is another option, a health-motivated segment may not continue to consume the product. This is exacerbated by attribution motivations, which can lead them to see themselves as having eaten the food because of health benefits and not because they enjoyed the food itself.

To understand why a person adopts an unfamiliar food for taste-related reasons, it is useful to profile those who have already adopted that type of food for taste-motivated reasons. Doing so can provide insights that can be used to identify the types of people who are most likely to adopt the food, and it can provide further insights into how to encourage such adoption.

The practical consequence of unlocking these correlates of taste-motivated consumption can be seen in the U.S. yogurt industry. In 1978, 7.8 percent of the population consumed 75 percent of yogurt. Although for most people it was a nutrition-motivated choice, for others the decision was taste motivated. Based on insights from this taste-motivated segment, companies such as Dannon and General Mills (Yoplait) focused their product development strategies on better-tasting yogurts. Per capita consumption doubled in the next decade, and yogurt is now a common food in many U. S. kitchens.

With yogurt, it was clear that a taste-motivated segment of yogurt lovers were responsible for driving innovation, new product introduction, and profitability in the early years of yogurt's growth. This taste-motivated segment also was largely responsible for the enthusiasm and the word-of-mouth persuasion that stimulated repeated trial among similarly predisposed but uninitiated nonusers of yogurt.

As an illustration for this chapter, consider soy. Today, soy is in a similar situation as yogurt was thirty years ago. Of the small percentage of Westerners who regularly and intentionally consume soy foods, the majority claim to do so because of its perceived health benefits, not its taste. Indeed, the belief that a product contains soy (even when it does not) has been shown to cause many nonvegetarian Americans to rate the taste of the product as grainy, chalky, dry, and unappealing, yet to also rate it as "tasting healthy."

To introduce the concept of taste-motivated segmentation, this chapter illustrates how the personality and behavior profile of a taste-motivated segment of soy consumers differs from a health-motivated segment and from a segment that does not regularly and knowingly consume soy. Developing these profiles can inform product development and communication strategies for firms that want to expand the consumption base for a new or unfamiliar food. More generally, these methods are appropriate for similar research with other underconsumed products (such as fruits and vegetables) or those produced or processed with unfamiliar techniques (such as those that have been genetically altered or irradiated).

What Differentiates a Taste-Motivated Segment from a Health-Motivated Segment?

To determine what characteristics might be associated with taste-motivated preferences for a product, qualitative and quantitative studies need to be conducted. Standard criteria have proved useful in profiling people who are predisposed to favoring specific foods (such as carbohydrate cravings) where there is evidence of these criteria. In most cases, however, existing scales and characteristics may not be known.

Results from Exploratory Qualitative Research

To illustrate this with soy, a qualitative study was conducted by Nasse (2001) with a convenience sample of thirty-three people who had clear preferences for soy foods and who had been recruited through fliers placed in a health food store, a regular supermarket, a health food restaurant, and a college cafeteria. Two focus groups were conducted (eight people each), and in-depth laddering interviews were conducted with the remaining seventeen participants. Each person was paid $20 for his or her participation. Although these people are not representative of the general population, the exploratory purpose was to generate ideas of what clusters of characteristics might differentiate them from people who did not consume soy in the general population. Given such insights, subsequent quantitative studies could be more fruitfully conducted with a more representative sample.

The results of this qualitative phase of the project indicated that the two major reasons people moved from infrequent to frequent consumption of soy foods (excluding soy dairy substitutes) were health-motivated reasons (such as heart disease concerns or high blood pressure) or taste-motivated reasons (they liked the taste or texture). Because our interest was primarily in those who ate these foods because of the taste, most of the subsequent qualitative work focused on determining clusters of similarities between these people. In addition to spending more time preparing food and enjoying fine dining, the people in this segment often claimed to be adventurous and to be opinion leaders among their peers.

Interestingly, these taste-motivated people often indicated that they would continue to eat soy even if it was not more healthful than an alternative. This is noteworthy because it suggests that these people might be likely to consume soy consistently over the long term because they see it not just as a means to an end (health) but rather as an end in itself (taste).

Results from Confirmatory Quantitative Research

To quantitatively examine these notions, Randy Westgren and I mailed a survey to 1,302 North American adults who were given a check for $6 in exchange for completing the study. Of those mailed surveys, 606 people (46.5 percent) promptly responded and were included in the study (63 percent female, average age forty-three years).

Each person was asked two broad types of questions that were directed at issues raised in the qualitative portion of the study. The first set of questions were related to how frequently each was involved in specific food-related behaviors in an average week. The second set asked them to agree or disagree with a series of personality-related statements (e.g., "I am traditional") that were asked on nine-point scales (1 = strongly disagree, 9 = strongly agree).

In the data analysis, consumers were categorized by whether they ate soy foods primarily for health reasons (23 percent) or for taste reasons (8 percent) or did not eat soy (69 percent). Some participants ate soy for both taste reasons and health reasons, and the more predominant of the two reasons was used to categorize these people.

As Figure 4.1 indicates, the profile of people who consumed soy for

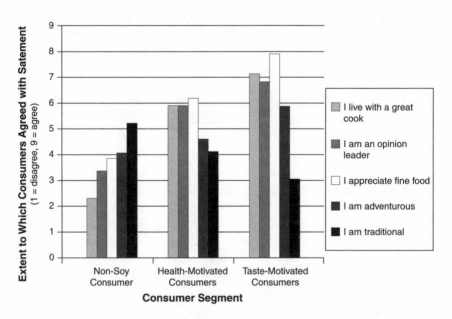

Figure 4.1. Taste-motivated consumers are different from health-motivated consumers.

taste reasons was consistently different from that of people who consumed it for health reasons. This was consistent with the findings of the qualitative portion of the study. That is, the taste-motivated consumers were more likely to believe they lived with a great cook than the health-motivated participants or the non–soy eating participants. In addition, compared with these other participants, they rated themselves as less traditional, more adventurous, and more likely to be opinion leaders.

In addition to these personality variables, taste-motivated participants ate evening meals away from home more often than the health-motivated and the non–soy eating participants. They also enjoyed wine with their meals more often. Both characteristics are consistent with what we might expect of people who appreciate a high-quality dining experience. Indeed, this group indicated that they were more "appreciative of fine food" than the other two segments.

Four Profiles of Motivated Soy Fanatics

The idea of profiling consumers is very powerful. If we can understand why some people like the taste of a particular functional food, then it might be possible to determine what we can do to encourage more people to consume it.

Let us now expand this example and develop more specific profiles of people who prepare and consume soy regularly. Profiling gives us the opportunity to generate hypotheses about the motivations and behaviors of individual consumers. The market insights gained from these profiling efforts are relevant to large segments of consumers and can help us develop a marketing strategy that communicates the benefits of soy to our target segments.

To develop such profiles, we conducted in-depth interviews among fifty American-born people who considered themselves taste-motivated lovers of soy. There was no time constraint, so interviewees could take as long as they needed to elaborate answers in their own words.

Signs, announcements, fliers, and direct mail efforts solicited volunteers who would be paid $40 to be interviewed. All communications specifically said that we were looking for people who had two characteristics in common. First, we needed taste-motivated consumers of soy who frequently and principally consumed it because they loved the taste of soy. Second, we needed people who regularly cooked soy-related meals. The reason we were interested in people who were active cooks is because of the disproportionate impact a good cook has over the eating habits of friends and family (see chapters 2 and 6).

Fifty eligible people (42 female) were selected and interviewed. Through a content analysis of the interviews, Nasse (2001) identified four general profiles of soy consumers: the Creative Cook, the Ethical Cook, the Carpe Diem Cook, and the Achiever Cook. There are two somewhat surprising observations about these profiles. First, although people were recruited because they claimed to be taste-motivated consumers of soy, two of the profiles were generally more health motivated. A second surprising observation was that all four groups were dominated by women. In general, however, there is nothing gender specific about any of these groups, yet for convenience I will use feminine pronouns to refer to these groups.

Although these are generalizations, they will prove useful in determining how to intelligently develop promotional efforts that will resonate with similar people who are not yet consumers of these foods. These profiles are summarized in Table 4.1, and discussed in terms of how marketing efforts can be used to communicate with others who are similar.

The Creative Cook (Taste Motivated)

The Creative Cook is young in spirit (and sometimes also in age). She likes soy foods for their taste and versatility. The bland taste of unflavored soy products is a challenge to her cooking creativity rather than a drawback. She is creative and enjoys artistic hobbies. Cooking helps relieve her stress, so she can accomplish more each day. She is interested in other cultures and values traditions. Self-esteem is also essential to her.

Products targeted at this type of consumer should have a firm texture; a soft texture was often perceived as undesirable in the interviews. Because Creative Cooks are less price sensitive than others, foods targeted toward them can be priced at a premium. These interviews suggest that soy foods can be distributed in supermarkets, gourmet food stores, and health stores. The promotions or the labeling associated with the products should emphasize the creativity of cooking with soy food and the healthful, natural image of soy.

The Ethical Cook (Taste Motivated)

The Ethical Cook is a female vegetarian. She purchases soy because she likes variety in her diet and likes soy's substantial texture and taste. Soy's texture and taste also allow her to experiment with it in the same way a

Table 4.1 Four Profiles of Motivated Consumers of Soy Foods

	The Creative Cook	The Ethical Cook	The Carpe Diem Cook	The Achiever Cook
Background	Female college student	Female vegetarian	Woman in her mid-thirties active in the community	Female college student
Reason for eating soy foods	Taste, versatility, health benefits	Needs variety and protein in her diet	Be healthier and have energy, stay slim	Health, convenience so she can focus on things other than foods
Self-perception	Creative, achiever, artistic, high self-esteem	More introspective than others, thinks about many things	Thin, very informed	Responsible, reliable, educated, and intelligent
General attitude	Grow up with interest in cultures; likes tradition and adding a personal touch to a meal	Feels strongly about a few issues and feels responsible for all her actions	A bit unconventional; thinks that knowledge and learning bring purpose to life and are fundamental to human nature	Likes to debate issues with others, hold intelligent conversations; her decisions are greatly influenced by a few key relationships
Social life	Needs to feel well-rounded	Not very social, a few close friends, very similar to her	Little time but loves spending time with her children	Friendly relations with peers, many friends to hang out with, close friends and family

Table 4.1 Cont.

	The Creative Cook	The Ethical Cook	The Carpe Diem Cook	The Achiever Cook
How this person wants to be seen	An artist and an achiever	Someone improving the world	Fun, attractive, very energetic, motivates others	Very active, important, useful, needed, successful
Hobbies	Cooking, painting, reading, nature	Being outdoors, feels very close to nature	Cooking ethnic foods, learning new things, outdoor activities	
Perception of other people's opinion		Not concerned but wants others to share her ideas	Not very concerned	Not concerned but wants to impress her family
How she/he spends her/his time	Less stress to achieve "longer days"	Alone, learning, exploring new ideas		Her free time is truly hers and is separated from work
Goals	Get a degree, feel good about self	Lofty goals, more subjective than objective	Interesting life; family	
What the neighbors may say about her/him		Withdrawn, difficult to talk to	Very successful, well educated, a bit different from most people	Hard worker, intelligent, fun-loving, witty

Source: Adapted from Nasse (2001).

person might cook meat. She sees herself as an introspective person who thinks about issues and their impact on all things and beings. She feels responsible for all of her actions and has strong opinions. She spends a lot of time alone and enjoys being outdoors because she feels close to nature. She cares more about improving the world than about success or other people's opinion of her.

According to these interviews, Ethical Cooks are interested in soy foods that are high in protein and variety. These soy foods should not be priced too high. The Ethical Cook sees the health properties of soy as a positive attribute. However, over a certain price she feels that she pays more for the healthful image than the real product. These interviews suggest that soy foods should be available in places such as health stores, co-ops, international specialty stores, and supermarkets. According to the interviews, promotions should emphasize the healthful and natural image of soy, and they should communicate such health benefits through health magazines and trusted third parties such as doctors and dietitians.

The Carpe Diem Cook (Health Motivated)

The Carpe Diem Cook wants to seize the day and make the most of it. She is a little older than the other prototypes of consumers, typically thirty-five to forty-five years. This person consumes soy foods to be slim, to be healthier, and to have energy for her family, her job, and all her activities in the community. She sees herself as attractive and well informed. She devotes a lot of time and effort to keeping informed about issues that affect her, such as nutrition. The small amount of free time she has is devoted to her family. She loves outdoor activities such as Frisbee, hiking, and picnicking and enjoys learning activities such as museums. The Carpe Diem Cook is a bit unconventional. She thinks that knowledge and learning bring purpose to life and are fundamental to human nature. She wants to live her life to the fullest. She does not care about other people's opinions of her.

The interviews suggest that the Carpe Diem Cook appreciates versatility and variety in soy foods. This consumer likes convenient products that are low in fat. Products designed for this segment should take these preferences into account. Because these women typically have young children, they would probably like new versions of popular soy foods packaged especially for children. The interviews suggested that the product must be a good value but need not be inexpensive. Supermarkets and traditional grocery stores seem to be appropriate places to sell soy foods. The Carpe

Diem Cook is ready to pay for the health benefits of soy foods. According to the interviews, direct sampling and communication on the health benefits of soy foods for the whole family would help reach this consumer segment. Promotions should focus on the nontraditional benefits of soy food for families on the go.

The Achiever Cook (Health Motivated)

The Achiever Cook is a younger version of the Carpe Diem Cook. She purchases soy foods because she wants to be healthy. She will do a healthful thing such as eating soy foods to "cancel out" a less healthful activity. She values convenience so she can put her efforts into things other than foods. She enjoys intellectual conversations and debates. It is very important for her to be able to use her free time as she wants and to separate it from work. The achiever perceives herself as a responsible, reliable, and intelligent person. She craves belonging. She does not care about most other people's opinions of her, with the exception of her family.

Although the Achiever Cook regularly cooks, cooking is simply a means to an end because she has little time to devote to food. Therefore, products targeted at this segment should be easy to use and come in large quantities. The package must be resealable and carry adequate guidelines. These features will allow the customer to save grocery trips and save time. Like the Carpe Diem Cook, the Achiever seems ready to purchase a "decent-value" product in her usual grocery store, but will pay a great deal more for convenience. This consumer segment reported the desire to eat soy foods to "cancel out" less nutritious foods. Therefore, placing soy snacks in the snack aisle and next to the cereal bars would position soy foods as a healthful alternative. According to the interviews, promotions should emphasize the health benefits of soy foods. Because having a sense of belonging is important for this segment, commercials should feature healthy people socializing.

Table 4.2 presents the main features of the marketing mix for each consumer segment that Nasse identified. For all segments, communicating the health benefits of soy foods would help increase consumption. Consumers also have to overcome their assumption that soy foods do not taste good. This could be achieved by trials and samples. These interviews suggest that soy foods should not be positioned as foods for vegetarian people because only one consumer segment is truly vegetarian. It seems that soy foods should be positioned as an alternative to more traditional foods and as part of a balanced diet. Furthermore, soy foods would be

Table 4.2. How the Marketing Mix Varies across Four Profiles of Motivated Soy Food Consumers

	The Creative Cook	The Ethical Cook	The Carpe Diem Cook	The Achiever Cook
Product	Firm texture; versatile soyfoods; variety of products	High in protein; versatility	Low in fat; versatile; variety of soyfoods; convenient; child packaging for popular adult soyfoods	Easy to use; resealable package; large quantities; adequate directions; no waste of time
Price	Not necessarily low; good value	Moderate to avoid the "health food" stereotype	Not necessarily low; good value	Not necessarily low; good value
Place	Health stores; gourmet food stores; supermarkets	Health stores; cafeterias, dorms; supermarkets	Supermarkets; traditional grocery stores	Next to cereal bars in supermarkets; snack aisle
Promotion	Emphasize versatility and the opportunity for creative cuisine; healthy, natural image; cooking books	Emphasize health benefits through magazines and third parties; healthy, natural image	Samples; focus on nontraditional aspect or "on-the-go" family; emphasize the health benefits for the whole family	A healthy alternative; show health benefits; commercials showing healthy people socializing

more widely adopted if they were available in group living places such as cafeterias and sorority houses.

The customer profiling technique illustrated here gives us a good idea of who is going to think soy tastes good. By taking a personalized walk in these interviewees' shoes, we have gained insights that can be generalized across a broader segment and may help us understand why the entire market segment consumes soy. With any functional food, if we can develop customer prototypes, we can better understand and therefore communicate our functional food products to specific audiences and win more ideal consumers.

Lessons for Marketing Nutrition

Many well-intended efforts to change nutrition-related behaviors have had disappointing results. Sixty years ago, efforts to encourage organ meat consumption in the protein-deficient rationing years of World War II were ineffective. Sixty years later, efforts to encourage increased soy and fruit and vegetable consumption in a calorie-rich but nutrient-deficient dietary environment are just as disappointing.

One exception to these disappointments is the success of yogurt. Yet even with yogurt, it is not clear that it would have become a popular food if taste-motivated segments had not been identified, understood, and nurtured thirty years ago. Doing so allowed the targeting of new product development strategies and more focused communication efforts that dramatically expanded its popularity and acceptance.

Although many efforts to change nutrition-related behaviors are directed toward a general population, this study suggests three important conclusions. First, some individuals or groups are more predisposed to changing their consumption behavior in a desired direction than others. Therefore, instead of encouraging all people to eat a food for health reasons, a more effective method may be to target the types of people who are more likely to prefer it for taste reasons. People who adopt foods for taste reasons may be more likely to continue with these dietary changes than those who simply do so for health reasons.

Second, targeting taste-oriented consumers can seed potential opinion leaders, who may eventually pass these dietary habits on to others either directly (through word of mouth) or indirectly. Who are these taste-predisposed segments? In the case of soy, they are most likely to live in a household with a good cook (generally them or their spouse) and to exhibit behaviors associated with food appreciation, such as dining out and drinking wine. These correlations are not necessarily causal, but they help us understand who can most effectively be targeted for at least the initial phases of a campaign focused on increasing soy consumption. Moreover, people who fit this profile of adventurous diners can be reached even more effectively through the burgeoning print and electronic media that are dedicated to nutrition and fine dining.

Third, good cooks are food gatekeepers for their families. They largely determine what family members eat at home, and their talent increases acceptance of foods they serve. Given this gatekeeping role, efforts to encourage the adoption of unfamiliar foods—whether they be yogurt in 1975 or soy today—would be more effective if directed at good cooks than at less proficient or less influential cooks. Although recent efforts have shown that these cooks can be divided into different subsegments based on their personality and their cooking-related behaviors, the next step should be to determine which of these subsegments is most predisposed to experimenting with and adopting unfamiliar foods.

Although people who eat soy for taste reasons do not necessarily eat soy as often as those who do so for health reasons, they may be the more loyal and consistent consumers of soy in the long run. In effect, instead of consuming soy as a means to an end, they consume it as an end in itself.

For anyone trying to increase the consumption of a functional food, whether a brand manager, a dietitian, or a public policy official, it is important to vividly picture or profile your audience before trying to communicate your ideas to them. This chapter explains that as we learn more about customers' wants, needs, interests, and attitudes, a detailed picture emerges of the ideal consumer. Although this profile is still a composite, it will help marketers uncover and understand who the potential consumers of the product are so that they can develop the most appropriate marketing mix.

If we can help people increase their consumption of functional foods such as soy, then we provide them with real options. These options may help developing countries combat protein deficiency. They can also be used to control Americans' growing waistlines. This chapter has given us more tools to use when building a marketing strategy around nutrition and functional foods. Directing nutritional education efforts at a general population will be much less effective than focusing on a more targeted group. Prototyping gives us the insights to segment our market and target people who are more likely to change their consumption behaviors in the first place. In any case, by communicating the benefits of functional foods and nutrition in a way that people can accept, we are helping people change their eating habits.

Related Readings

There are two key elements to this chapter. The first is the basic method of profiling; the second involves the more specific findings related to the context of soy. Three of the following articles (Wansink 1994c, 1997, 2000) provide a useful background on how to profile (or prototype) perfect consumers. The other three are soy specific and can be useful as templates for other functional foods.

Nasse, Laure. "Modeling the Future Acceptance of Soy Products." Unpublished master's thesis, University of Illinois at Urbana, 2001.

Wansink, Brian. "Developing and Validating Useful Consumer Prototypes." *Journal of Targeting, Measurement and Analysis for Marketing* 3:1 (1994c): 18–30.

———. "Developing Accurate Customer Usage Profiles." In *Values, Lifestyles, and Psychographics*. Ed. Lynn Kahle. 183–98. Cambridge, MA: Lexington, 1997.

———. "New Techniques to Generate Key Marketing Insights." *Marketing Research* (Summer 2000): 28–36.

Wansink, Brian, and JaeHak Cheong. "Taste Profiles That Correlate with Soy Consumption in Developing Countries." *Pakistan Journal of Nutrition* 1:6 (December 2002): 276–78.

Wansink, Brian, and Randall E. Westgren. "Profiling Taste-Motivated Segments." *Appetite,* 41 (2004): 323–27.

FIVE

Mental Maps That Lead to Consumer Insights

We know that people have different attitudes about food, but how are these attitudes influenced? Several factors, such as food preferences, beliefs, values, socioeconomic status, and knowledge of nutrition, influence the formation of food attitudes. Understanding why and how people choose the foods they do will help us develop a more targeted marketing communication strategy and ultimately influence their eating behavior.

One way to do this is by drawing mental maps. Mental maps represent how different characteristics of a food are associated with one another. That is, when a person thinks of blueberries, she might think of them as low in calories and healthful. In turn, she might associate low calorie and healthy with blueberry's being nutritious, and she might then associate eating nutritiously with being a good parent and being an energetic and attractive person. In the end, the simplified mental map described here would show that eating a low-calorie, healthful food such as blueberries points to the person wanting to be a good parent and an energetic and attractive person. A number of examples of mental maps are provided throughout this chapter.

Mental maps are developed based on the insights that one gets when conducting laddering interviews. A laddering interview is similar to the classic picture of a psychologist interviewing a patient on a couch, gaining insights into the patient's life that are not easily apparent. The psychologist is trying to get to the root of the problem through questioning. Laddering serves the same function, with the exception that the marketer is not searching for the root of a problem. Rather, he or she is trying to find the root reasons for the customer's purchase of a particular food. In contrast to surveys, which trace or assess general consumer sentiment, laddering assesses deeper reasons why individual consumers buy. Aggregating these deep perceptions allows more profound but still generalizable insights to be uncovered.

When customers perceive personal relevance in a product's attributes, it is because the product becomes more strongly and uniquely associated with desirable usage consequences. This chapter presents laddering as a useful method for evaluating means-end theory and generating consumer insights that help guide marketing strategy and execution.

Mental Maps and the Laddering Technique

Mental maps are the hierarchical organization of consumer perceptions and product knowledge (Gutman 1982) that range from attributes to consumption consequences to personal values (attributes → consequences → values). This basic hierarchy starts with product attributes that have consumption consequences (e.g., the "low calorie" attribute of celery having the consequence of controlling weight or the vitamin A attribute of a carrot having the consequence of improving eyesight). Each consequence, in turn, supports one or more important values in that person's life. Means-end theory seeks to understand human actions—in this case food consumption—as a means of satisfying different levels of needs. Means-end theory suggests that concrete attributes link to self-relevance and more abstract associations. Laddering is an effective way to evaluate and draw implications about the means-end theory.

Laddering uses a series of progressive questions that allow an interviewer to understand how a product's attributes, the consequences of using it, and the personal values it satisfies are linked together. Attributes are the physical properties of the product. Consequences are outcomes, derived from attributes, that the customer associates with the use of the product. Values are derived from associations between consequences and personal value systems. Values, often attributed to deep emotional needs, often represent the real reason why people buy high-equity brands. On Maslow's hierarchy of needs, values are on a higher level than product attributes and consequences. The strength of associations between attributes, consequences, and values has a strong influence on favorable intentions toward buying a product.

Attributes Only Scratch the Surface

When first asked why they purchase a product, consumers typically answer in simple, superficial ways. These responses sound right to the consumer, but they reveal little about the reasons for the purchase. These responses often describe attributes of the product, such as taste, price, size, brand name, quality, and price or value. Although they may describe the product accurately, they are seldom the *real* reasons why people buy products. Past experiences in interviewing target consumers for various products generated some examples that illustrate how consumers initially answer with attribute-level responses. Consider the following quotations from different sets of interviews with women thirty-five to forty-five years old with two or more children at home.

1. "Carrots are a great snack, particularly in those resealable bags."
2. "Cranberries add a kick to things and are healthy for me."
3. "I like to eat honey because it tastes good and it fills me up in the morning, so I'm not hungry an hour later."

Each of these explanations does little more than describe the physical characteristics of the product. However, it is from these attributes that an interviewer can begin to move toward the values behind these purchases through probing questions that examine some of the consequences consumers associate with these attributes.

Consequences Provide Key Insights

The next step in finding the values affecting a purchasing decision is to examine why the attribute-level distinction is important to the individual. This begins to reveal more personal reasons for purchasing a product rather than describing the physical characteristics of the product. Consumers associate certain attributes with the relevant consequences of eating that food, and the purchase decision may result from hopes of achieving these associated consequences. Often the insights gained here can be directly applied to formulating an effective education or marketing campaign. To continue our example, consider the follow-up questions and answers to the three examples noted earlier:

1. "Carrots are a great snack, particularly in those resealable bags."
   What do you mean by a "great snack"?
   "Well, it takes my mind off of hunger without making me feel guilty or without giving me a sugar rush. They also last longer."
2. "Cranberries add a kick to things and are healthy for me."
   Why is it important for a food to "add a kick" to you?
   "It makes me feel more full and satiated. I don't feel like I'm sacrificing."
3. "I like to eat honey because it tastes good and it fills me up in the morning, so I'm not hungry an hour later."
   Why is it important that you are not hungry an hour later?
   "First of all, I have more energy and tend to get more accomplished at my job. Also, not having to stop work to eat something keeps me working and I get more done at work."

Asking "Why?" to a customer's initial answers results in statements that begin to reveal more about the abstract and emotional qualities the customer associates with the brand. These are not merely statements about the product but rather thoughtful personal reflections that are one step closer to the personal values that drive the purchase. Consequences specify the way a value is linked to an attribute of the product. Consequences are the key component of an effective education and marketing platform. It is from the consequences of a laddering interview that such campaigns are developed.

Often, a consumer reveals many consequences about something he or she has eaten. Questions are continually asked until a value is revealed. This value may present itself after as few as two questions or as many as twenty questions. The process depends on the questions asked and the consumer's involvement with the product. An interviewer should not expect to find a consumer's personal values behind a purchase in three abrupt questions. Usually, it takes thirty to forty minutes for each interview to gain significant results.

Values Are the Real Reason People Buy

The reasons for purchasing decisions are not always apparent. Although consumers will quickly respond to product-related questions, their responses often are not their core reasons for purchasing a product. Often consumers are not even aware of these core reasons. Most often, in-depth questioning reveals these core reasons for purchasing a product. When consumers buy, they attempt to self-justify the purchase in order to maintain cognitive consistency. When a person buys a high-equity brand, he or she often buys it because it fills an emotional need as well as a practical one. For example, when a consumer was asked why he bought Pocari Sweat, an imported Japanese sport drink, his initial responses included the facts that it was imported and had a fancy label. After further questioning, however, it was found that his real reasons for purchasing the imported drink were a sense of exclusiveness, personal well-being, and important memories of long-term friends that are evoked through the purchase. Values such as these are related at some level to most product purchases. Seven of the most common general values that influence the purchase of food are accomplishment, belonging, self-fulfillment, self-esteem, family, satisfaction, and security. With the exception of security, most of these values can be associated with the social and self-actualization levels of Maslow's hierarchy of needs.

Using Laddering to Develop Mental Maps

The object of a laddering interview is to uncover how product attributes, usage consequences, and personal values are linked in a person's mind. Doing so will help create a meaningful mental map of the consumer's view toward the target product, and by combining the maps of similar consumers, one can develop a large, more exhaustive map.

The mental map is a graphic description of a laddering interview that illustrates the relationships between the attributes, consequences, and values. Each attribute, consequence, and value is found by questioning the interviewee based on previous responses. This allows the interviewer to slowly "climb the ladder" (from attributes to consequences to values) to get to the real reason a person buys a given product. Figure 5.1 is a mental map for flavored yogurts.

Laddering provides a way of getting past the superficial to what is really

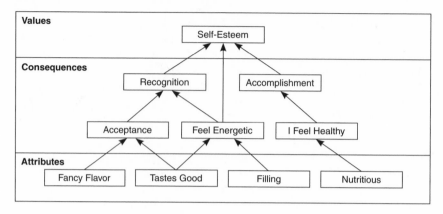

Figure 5.1. Hierarchical value map for flavored yogurts.

important. This chapter provides a framework for conducting a laddering interview.

The first step in effective laddering is to choose a "food champion," someone who is loyal to the food and is enthusiastic about promoting it. Although this person is not representative of the population, recall that the purpose of the laddering interview is to understand the real benefits a person gets from a food and to use this knowledge to better promote consumption of the food. The best way to uncover the core associations is to talk to someone who feels strongly about the food. Interviewing casual users or convenience-oriented "fair weather" purchasers will provide too few insights as to what food attributes can be built upon and leveraged.

Although the goal of the laddering interview is to determine the abstract, possibly subconscious reasons for purchase behavior, the interview begins with questions that allow the brand champion to talk about the product's attributes. The consequences that are revealed along the way become the key insights used in a marketing strategy. Consider the following questions:

- How often do you eat this food?
- What do you like about this food?
- What do you eat when you're tired of this food?
- Tell me about the most recent time you ate this food.

The purpose of this first round of questions is to determine what attributes or properties of the food cause the interviewee to purchase and champion it. Once several attributes of the food have been identified and questioning becomes repetitive, it is time to move on.

Before beginning questioning again, review the answers to the initial questions. Subsequent questions should be based on these answers. In this manner, a ladder or mental map is constructed, establishing links between the attributes, consequences, and values. The interviewer asks why an attribute is important in the second round of questions. Inquiries about attributes elicit answers about consequences. Questions that investigate consequences in turn elicit the underlying personal values, the real reasons why the purchased was made. The interviewee must reflect on the purchase, so it is important to continue questioning along the same vein. Stopping and returning to a consequence at a later time often causes the interviewee to lose his or her train of thought about a given consequence.

Finding the right questions to ask in any given interview can be done only through experience. Table 5.1 offers a few tips for conducting an interview. It is important to note that the questions mentioned in this chapter are merely a sample of questions that were compiled in doing the

Table 5.1. Suggestions for Conducting of Laddering Interviews

Facilitation Techniques	Actions to Avoid
Ask questions that would reveal personal reasons	Don't rush
Ask questions that cause a person to think and respond with a sentence, not yes/no	Don't ask questions that can be answered in one word
Ask "Why?"	Don't force the interviewee to answer the question in a certain way
Question a person's reasons for their responses	Don't expect to get to a value in three questions
Allow the questioning to flow, even if the questions are not directly brand related	Don't assume that a person means something other than what they say
Ask questions that give the interviewee free reign to answer the question as they see fit	Don't force the issue; some of the consequences may not lead to where you want to go; change topics and start again
Watch the person's face as they answer the question and listen to the tone in their voice	

Source: Wansink (2003e).

interviews for this study. Practice and experience determine what questions should be asked at any given moment during the interview.

How About an Example?

We have examined why laddering can be useful in developing a marketing campaign for nutrition or a particular functional food. When applied to consumers of functional food, laddering provides key insights as to why these consumers choose to eat what they do. We can apply this laddering technique to learn more about consumers' behavior toward any functional food. The resulting mental maps can describe how people form their attitudes toward a food, and these insights can then be applied to a detailed marketing mix that best relates to consumers' values. As an illustration, let's consider soy users.

In an effort to learn more about soy users, a group of soy consumers were interviewed using a laddering technique to reveal several attributes, consequences, and values related to soy (Nasse 2001). As expected, when consumers were asked, "Why do you like soy?" most answers were attributes, such as "It has protein," "It has a good taste," or "It's pretty convenient." All of these answers were descriptions of the product. Continuing to ask "why" questions revealed more abstract and emotional responses rather than just mere descriptors. Continued responses showed consequences such as "I consume less" or "It's good for my cholesterol." Continued probing can help respondents think of higher-level values associated with those consequences.

In the responses of fifty interviewees, many elements or answers were mentioned multiple times. By noting which elements have the highest frequency, we can begin to understand which attribute-consequence-value chains are most relevant. The most important attributes respondents mentioned are "taste," "healthy food," "protein," "convenience," and "vegetarian." Key consequences included "energy," "accomplish more," "maintain health and balanced diet," "mental activity/challenge," "no worries, safe," "responsible/control over life," and "enhance and build your personality." The laddering interviews revealed the core values of "self-esteem," "achievement," "happiness," "live life to the fullest," and "belonging." This means that these consumers are eating soy, and view soy, as a means to achieve their goals for attaining those higher-level values.

We find that there is a strong relationship between responses if many respondents mention similar attribute-consequence-value chains. With our results from the laddering, three important relationship chains emerged that will be discussed separately for the sake of simplicity. We will discuss the "healthy food–self-esteem" chain, the "convenience-happiness" chain, and the "cost-happiness" chain. The elements of the chains were arranged in the most logical order to form chains that would reflect all the steps of the interviews without creating redundancy between the sets of chains.

What the Chains Reveal

The "healthy food–self esteem" chain reveals a segment of consumers who take care of their physical appearance and see soy as a way to achieve this goal. These people want to have a healthy, fit body that makes them feel good and gives them high self-esteem. These consumers responded first by saying they like soy for its protein content, or because it's healthful. But the real reason this tool is so useful to dietitians, brand managers, and health professionals is that it reveals deeper insights into why that attribute is important to the consumer. Notice in Figure 5.2 that the attributes

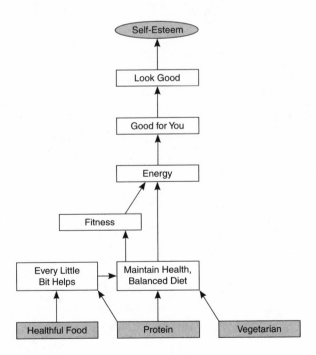

Figure 5.2. Health food–self-esteem chain.

of soy are important to these consumers because consumption leads to positive consequences of eating soy. These consequences include "eating soy makes me feel energetic, fit, and look good." These consequences are important because for this segment, eating soy ultimately helps them achieve a higher value in their life: self-esteem. When communicating to consumers about soy, we can better relate to them if we understand how they think and why they think what they do.

Another important chain that emerged was the "convenience-happiness" chain. Respondents in this group felt soy was convenient and easy to use in food preparation. Expanding on these responses, we learn that convenience has a number of positive consequences; it allows easy preparation in food and adds more food choices. Following the chain upward toward higher values, we see that the trail of consequences leads to happiness and a sense of belonging and accomplishment. Eating soy is consistent with these consumers' goals and higher values.

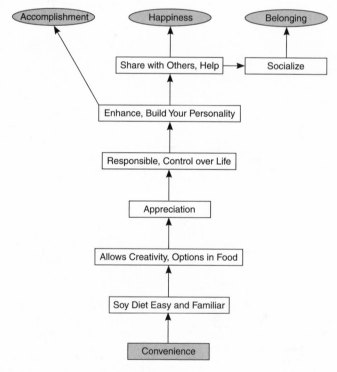

Figure 5.3. Convenience-happiness chain.

A final segment of consumers are characterized by the "cost-happiness" chain. These respondents use soy in a way that ultimately helps them achieve happiness. By following the path of this chain, we can begin to understand why consumers in this segment choose soy. At first, these consumers mentioned cost to be the most important attribute. Many of these respondents also said that along with cost, convenience was important to them. Following the consumers' logic for eating soy, we learn that saving money and time increases their independence. These people see eating soy as a cost saver that increases their independence, which leads to accomplishment.

Lessons for Marketing Nutrition

When we try to understand consumer behavior, we often wonder where to turn next; sometimes we turn to past research, sometimes to surveys, sometimes to focus groups, and sometimes to intuition. In most situations, the best method is to listen to the consumer while doing a little investigative work with "why" questions. From this we can truly understand the higher values associated with their food decisions. This chapter provides a tool that helps us to understand the minds of consumers. If you're reading this book, you probably wonder how you can make a notable impact in people's diets or food choices. Mental mapping provides the best way to communicate our ideas in the most relevant way to our audience. When we start reaching consumers effectively, we begin to make an impact on their behavior.

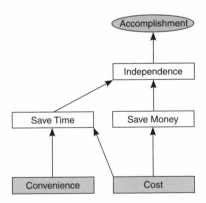

Figure 5.4. Cost-happiness chain.

This method of understanding consumer food choice is an important tool for communicating the benefit of nutrition. Whether you're a dietitian trying to help clients to eat properly, a health professional recommending diets, or a brand manager communicating the importance of a particular functional food, understanding how people form attitudes about the food they eat is the first step in making a change in a person's diet.

In this chapter, we applied the laddering technique to discover the reasons why people eat soy. This technique can be applied to understanding any consumer food choice. Soy is a particularly interesting example because it is becoming more popular in the United States. An increasing variety of soy food is available in the supermarket, and consumers are gradually losing their reluctance to try soy foods. By laddering, we were able to identify characteristics of soy foods that are relevant to consumers and distinguish several segments of consumers through an attribute-consequence-value chain model. When we communicate our ideas about nutrition, we must consider what is relevant to different segments and have special approaches for each segment.

Related Readings

Details on how to use laddering to gain insights about other foods can be found in the first two articles. The last resource offers a richly detailed investigation of laddering in the context of soy consumers.

Nasse, Laure. "Modeling the Future Acceptance of Soy Products." Unpublished master's thesis, University of Illinois, Urbana, 2001.

Wansink, Brian. "New Techniques to Generate Key Marketing Insights." *Marketing Research* (Summer 2000): 28–36.

Wansink, Brian. "Using Laddering to Understand and Leverage a Brand's Equity." *Qualitative Market Research: An International Journal* 6:2 (2003e): 111–18.

SIX

Targeting Nutritional Gatekeepers

The biggest single driver of consumption is the availability of a particular food. In most households, what is eaten for breakfast, lunch, dinner, and snacks is determined by what the primary grocery shopper—the food gatekeeper—has purchased. If a teenager wants to eat Pop-Tarts but they are not in the house, he or she will probably not eat Pop-Tarts. The teenager would have to make a separate trip to the grocery store, borrow some from a neighbor, or persuade the gatekeeper to buy them on the next shopping trip.

If only rice cakes are available, the teenager must decide whether to eat them, but this is a constrained decision. The primary grocery shopper determines what can be consumed in the house when he or she buys groceries. Most of us believe that we determine our food choices, but the set of options we have is determined by whoever does the shopping. Even when we consider what people eat when away from home (be they sack lunches or school lunches), our surveys indicate that about 72 percent of the food decisions by family members are made directly or indirectly by the primary grocery shopper and food preparer. It has been found that the actions and enthusiasm of the gatekeepers can help develop beliefs and preferences about food.

For the purposes of marketing nutrition, this is good news because it means that we do not have to convince every man, woman, teenager, and child to eat more nutritiously. All we need to do is to convince the food gatekeeper for the family. Typically (approximately 87 percent of the time) this gatekeeper is also the person who has the prime responsibility for food preparation. Research since the 1940s has shown that family members are likely to eat what the gatekeeper buys and prepares. Trying to convince the entire country to eat more fruits and vegetables, for instance, would not be as productive as simply convincing the primary shopper of the household to buy more fruits and vegetables and fewer processed foods.

We also know from the previous chapters that one of the common elements among taste-motivated people was that they claimed to live with a great cook. There are benefits of focusing only on the primary meal planners because they are more serious about this role. The influence of these good cooks is much higher than that of convenience cooks or carry-out cooks. Past work shows that these good cooks were more effective in encouraging their families to consume organ meats during the rationing years of World War II (chapter 2). Even today, recent studies show that people who like the taste of soy often indicate that they live with a good cook (see chapter 4).

Given the influence good cooks can have on long-term eating habits, nutrition marketers must develop effective methods that categorize the cooks that are most predisposed to nutrition-related behavior. This chapter examines two questions: Which domain—cooking behavior, food usage, or personality—best differentiates between various subsegments of good cooks? What types of cooks can most easily be persuaded to adopt healthier foods and healthier lifestyles?

After providing a background on common and distinct characteristics of good cooks, this chapter looks at ways to categorize these characteristics and determine which are most related to adopting healthier foods. If the goal is to encourage consumers to eat more of a functional food, these categorizations can help reveal which types of cooks would be the most promising to target. Identifying these traits and marketing specifically toward these segments is the most efficient means of communicating a nutrition-related message.

Good cooks who serve as gatekeepers are defined as primary meal planners who prepare favorable food for their families. Such cooks often describe themselves as being better than average cooks and are referred to by others as better than average. Yet not all cooks are the same. There are very different types of good cooks, and there are a number of dimensions on which they can be defined.

Studies that follow the development of master chefs—people who are good cooks—most commonly note several characteristic domains. We will look at three domains in which gatekeepers might be differentiated: their cooking behavior, their food usage, and their personality.

Distinguishing Characteristics of the Gatekeeper: Categorizing Nutritional Gatekeepers

Biographies of passionate chefs indicate high levels of ambition, creativity, experimentation, and hard work. These characteristics of professional cooks are not very different from those of their amateur counterparts. Good cooks often are adventurous, creative, ambitious, and willing to try new foods in ways that will enhance their enjoyment of cooking. However, one cook may be well liked and lighthearted, and another cook may be dominant and competitive. This suggests that personality characteristics may also be used to differentiate cooks.

To develop a set of scales that can be used to differentiate cooks, we used a two-stage process. First, we gave questionnaires to eighty-seven people between the ages of twenty-three and eighty-two, asking them to describe their personality, the foods they had cooked for dinner in the past two weeks, and the ways in which they had cooked and entertained in the past month. We then asked questions about how skilled they were and asked them to differentiate themselves from other cooks they knew. Finally, we asked a series of scale questions to validate and clarify their qualitative responses.

Second, we conducted a series of demographically matched focus groups of self-classified good cooks, bad cooks, and a mixed group to better understand the differentiating characteristics related to personality, behavior, and food usage.

Finally, we conducted a national survey of 2,000 people to obtain information on cooks and their lifestyles. We used the survey to identify those who are the primary shoppers and meal planners in their households. After completing the survey, participants were asked to rate their personality traits on nine-point scales. Health-related personality traits and food usage were used to examine health tendencies of cooks and responses to novel foods.

We divided the survey into groups of questions related to cooking behaviors, food usage, personality, cooking proficiency, nutritional predispositions, and demographics. To differentiate good cooks from average or below-average cooks, we asked a series of questions on comparative and absolute levels. We found significant characteristics that allowed us to differentiate the two segments. For example, good cooks are more actively involved in cooking activities such as trying more new recipes, having more cookbooks, using more spices, having more guests over for dinner, and making more casseroles. Also, good cooks are more likely to cook by instinct and describe themselves as creative cooks. These results lend further support to the distinction between good and average cooks, and they motivate further analysis based on this distinction.

A number of target measures are of interest in promoting adoption of new foods and establishing of healthful eating behaviors. In prior studies of functional food adoption, four important characteristics were whether a person was socially influential, inclined toward healthful behavior, predisposed to new foods, and eager to learn (Hunt and Hillsdon 1996). The relationship of these factors with various behavioral, food usage, and personality measures, indicates what domain best differentiates dimensions of good cooks that relate most closely to target behaviors.

As a general note, these cooks estimated that, on average, they were directly or indirectly responsible for approximately 72 percent of the food eaten by their families. A large part of their influence was direct and was based on the food they purchased and the food they prepared for meals and snacks. Another part of their influence was indirect and was based on how much of the food money their children and spouses spent away from home had been influenced by their suggestions or by the example set at home.

Why is this important? If we can obtain a detailed understanding of who these cooks are, how they behave, and what foods they like to cook with, we can be better-informed marketers and create marketing campaigns specifically tailored to these cooks. The best marketing campaigns reach their customers by specifically targeting the core audience. If we want to become better nutrition marketers, we need to be able to specifically target our audiences. This chapter shows us how our gatekeeper audience varies by behavior, food usage, and personality so that we can use this information to tailor our own marketing program.

Segmenting Cooks by Cooking Behavior

In analyzing good cooks on the basis of their cooking behavior, we found three distinct behavior categories: the New Recipe Cook, the Inventive Cook, and the Social Occasion Cook (see Wansink 2002 for additional details).

New Recipe Cooks try a wide variety of recipes but almost exclusively use cookbooks. They cook for enjoyment, often preparing food to satisfy only their own tastes rather than various tastes of a large group.

Inventive Cooks view cooking as a hobby and often experiment with new recipes. However, they use their instincts to create their own combinations of foods and techniques, and they enjoy unpredictable outcomes. They cook to satisfy the tastes of themselves and one or two others; they are not concerned about satisfying the diverse tastes of groups.

Social Occasion Cooks prepare large meals (sometimes using the oven to cook casseroles) that aim to please a wide variety of tastes found in a social gathering. To avoid the risk of making large dishes that do not satisfy guests, social cooks rely on standard recipes. Rather than treating cooking as a hobby, they use cooking as a social mediator, a facilitator of acceptance, belonging, and affection. For them, cooking behavior is related less to the motivation to cook than to the associated social benefits and social identity.

This provides a basis on which to differentiate cooks. Interestingly, we find that Social Occasion Cooks are socially influential but are not predisposed to trying new foods. Both New Recipe Cooks and Inventive Cooks are predisposed to trying new foods but are not particularly socially influential. What differentiates them is that the former needs the recipe, whereas the later needs only the inspiration.

Segmenting Cooks by Food Usage

When we analyzed cooks on the basis of food usage, three categories emerged: the Meat-Focused Cook, the Vegetable-Focused Cook, and the Self-Regulated Cook.

The consumption of beef, chicken, and pork was the most important characteristic distinguishing *Meat-Focused Cooks*. The *Vegetable-Focused Cook* has five or more fruits or vegetables each day, and she or he often serves broccoli. Finally, *Self-Regulated Cooks* are people who eat dessert after dinner and drink milk every day. Self-Regulated Cooks use rules or rituals to set a regular pattern for their lives. This category differs from the other identified categories because it focuses on behavior patterns, whereas the other categories focus on the content of the diet.

Although food usage can indicate what flavors a cook prefers when he or she prepares food, it does not differentiate segments of cooks as well as behavioral and personality characteristics. The study showed few food usage characteristics systematically differentiated good cooks. One reason was because the use of many different foods (e.g., endive, anchovies, leeks) was so sporadic that they did not produce consistent differences. Although this resulted in a small number of segments, it also reflects the potential difficulties in trying to differentiate cooks based on their food usage.

Segmenting Cooks by Personality

Segmenting cooks by personality was more rich (and complex) than segmenting cooks solely on their cooking behaviors and food usage. For this reason, a more detailed treatment will be given to personality and its implications for healthful behaviors and nutrition-related marketing.

A cluster analysis showed that six primary personality segments made up 90.8 percent of all cooks surveyed: *Giving Cooks* (21.3 percent), *Innovative Cooks* (20.7 percent), *Competitive Cooks* (16.3 percent), *Methodical Cooks* (15.7 percent), *Healthy Cooks* (10.2 percent), and *Athletic Cooks* (6.6 percent).

Table 6.1 shows what personality traits are associated with these six major segments. The numbers in this table indicate how strongly various personality traits relate to the people in each segment. The more strongly the trait is associated with the segment, the higher the number (up to 1.0). This table shows that a wide variety of personality traits are associated with cooks. To treat these cooks as homogeneous would be a mistake.

Interestingly, the characteristics of these different cooks are related to different nutrition-related behaviors that can make them influential gatekeepers. Consumers were asked questions about four behaviors of interest in changing food habits. These relate to the extent to which people perceive themselves as socially influential, inclined toward healthful habits, predisposed toward new foods, and eager to learn new ideas.

The last column in Table 6.1 also shows which of these four health-related behaviors (if any) is most strongly related to each personality trait. Viewed differently, we can also take each of these personality traits and examine which cooks are most associated with these behaviors:

—People who are socially influential tend to be friendly, well liked, outgoing, giving, enthusiastic, trend setting, nurturing, and initiating. These characteristics correspond most closely to *Giving Cooks* and to a lesser extent to *Innovative Cooks, Competitive Cooks,* and *Methodical Cooks.*

Table 6.1. Personality Traits That Relate to Six Segments of Good Cooks and to Nutrition-Related Behavior

	Giving Cooks (21.3%)	Innovative Cooks (20.7%)	Healthy Cooks (10.2%)	Athletic Cooks (6.6%)	Competitive Cooks (16.3%)	Methodical Cooks (15.7%)	Nutrition-Related Behavior Most Highly Related to This Personality Trait
Real friendly	.83						Socially influential
Well liked	.81						Socially influential
Outgoing	.76						Socially influential
"Giver"	.70						Socially influential
Enthusiastic	.68						Socially influential
Light-hearted	.63						Socially influential
Witty	.60						Socially influential
Nurturing	.50						Socially influential
Innovator		.86					Eager to learn
Thinks differently		.69					Eager to learn
Trendsetter		.68					Predisposed toward new foods
Creative		.61					Predisposed toward new foods
Curious		.49					Socially influential
Imaginative		.49					Socially influential
Initiator		.47					Socially influential
Healthy			.68				Inclined toward healthy behavior
Reader			.56				Eager to learn
Optimistic			.51				Eager to learn
Athletic				.73			Inclined toward healthy behavior
Nature lover				.72			Inclined toward healthy behavior
Earthy				.65			Inclined toward healthy behavior
Dominant					.79		Socially influential
Competitive					.68		Socially influential
Impulsive					.50		Predisposed toward new foods
Adventuresome					.43		Socially influential
Methodical						.76	Not Socially influential
Cultured						.45	Eager to learn

Note: These personalities comprise 90.8% of the good cooks studied. For parsimony, healthy and athletic cooks can be combined.

—People who are inclined toward healthful behavior tend to be healthy, nature lovers, athletes, and earthy. Unsurprisingly, these characteristics correspond most closely to *Healthy Cooks* and *Athletic Cooks.*

—People who are predisposed toward new foods are impulsive, curious, imaginative, adventurous, and innovative. These characteristics correspond most closely to *Innovative Cooks* and to a lesser extent to *Competitive Cooks.*

—People who are eager to learn new ideas are readers, optimistic, cultured, curious, imaginative, self-sufficient, and flexible. These characteristics correspond most closely to *Innovative Cooks, Healthy Cooks,* and *Methodical Cooks.*

In an effort to encourage gatekeepers to adopt a functional food, it would not be wise to target all cooks or even all good cooks. If the four nutrition-related behaviors are characteristic of a potential soy adopter, then the ideal segments of cooks to target are not just the *Healthy Cooks* and the *Athletic Cooks.* They are also the *Innovative Cooks, Competitive Cooks,* and *Methodical Cooks.*

Lessons for Marketing Nutrition

Research on the rationing years of the 1940s showed that good cooks can have a notable impact as nutritional gatekeepers (chapter 2). It did not show the criteria on which different types of cooks could be classified and which segments of these cooks were most influential. This chapter showed that cooks can be categorized most effectively by personality. Six primary personality types were found to make up 90.8 percent of all good cooks: *Giving Cooks, Innovative Cooks, Healthy Cooks, Athletic Cooks, Competitive Cooks,* and *Methodical Cooks.*

On average, these cooks estimated that they were directly or indirectly responsible for approximately 72 percent of the food eaten by their families. A large part of their influence was direct and was based on the food they purchased and the food they prepared for meals and snacks. Another part of their influence was indirect and was based on how much they influenced the discretionary food choices their children and spouses make away from home. This influence could be in the form of suggestions or in the example set at home.

To target nutritional gatekeepers, such as good cooks, in an education campaign, it is important to realize that they are not all the same. Such campaigns should be targeted at the most relevant and influential segments of this group. For instance, if the goal is to encourage consumers to eat an unfamiliar functional food, certain personality segments would be most promising to target. *Innovative Cooks* are likely to be most interested in novel foods and are also likely to be socially influential. *Healthy Cooks* are most likely to be eager to learn. In contrast, *Giving Cooks,* though socially influential, appear to have few other traits that would make us believe they would adopt a novel, healthful food.

Past efforts to study nutrition education have focused primarily on the consumer. But gatekeeper research from the 1940s suggests that cooks are also responsible for nutrition, as both gatekeepers and opinion leaders. Past efforts to target opinion leaders for nutrition change involved targeting cooks who are healthy or athletic. If an effort to encourage the use of a functional food is to be targeted at opinion-leading, gatekeeping cooks, a broad education effort aimed at all cooks would be too general, and a narrow education effort aimed at only Healthy or Athletic Cooks would be too restrictive. The best campaign would also target *Innovative Cooks, Competitive Cooks, Stimulation-Seeking Cooks,* and *Methodical Cooks.*

The more we know about consumers, the better we are able to tailor our marketing message to them. Typically, nutrition education has been targeted at the eaters of the food; this study shows that it may be worthwhile to consider specific marketing messages directed toward the cooks.

Personality characteristics are the most differentiating and nutrition-related characteristics. Indeed, Table 6.1 indicates how differentiated the largest of these five segments are in terms of personality. Marketers of functional foods can use this information to design a specifically targeted marketing campaign that would most effectively increase the adoption of their functional food. Not all cooks are the same. They do not make the same food choices, and they do not have the same motivations. Treating all these cooks as homogeneous will be ineffective because it will not speak to who they are and why they do what they do. Targeting them with different messages through different communication channels allows less costly, more compelling marketing efforts.

Related Readings

This chapter has been based in part on the following article, which describes the methods and findings in much more detail.

Wansink, Brian. "Profiling Nutritional Gatekeepers: Three Methods for Differentiating Influential Cooks." *Food Quality and Preference* 14:4 (June 2003d): 289–97.

PART THREE

The Health of Nations

SEVEN

The De-marketing of Obesity

People want a variety of high-value, tasty foods that they can have in large quantities whenever they want. Years of evolution and learned behavior have led people away from eating foods that are less palatable and less convenient to obtain. This is one reason overeating at McDonald's is so much easier to do than convincing children to eat broccoli.

Although they cater to our biological interests, food companies have recently been accused of contributing to the growing problem of obesity in the United States. Because of our basic predisposition toward eating plentiful amounts of sweet and fattening foods, these companies have been accused of responding to a super-sized problem by throwing gasoline on the fire.

Marketers are torn between two primary groups of stakeholders. One group consists of consumers who want a variety of tasty, inexpensive, convenient food, and the other consists of concerned public policy officials and activists who believe that companies should be more responsive in helping combat obesity. With their concern comes the potential threat of boycotts, activism, taxes, fines, restrictions, and legislation. The threat of being the tobacco industry of the new millennium is not trivial for consumer packaged-goods companies and fast-foods firms.

Although the situation appears perplexing, there are reasonable solutions. Food companies and marketers who have succeeded have done so by creating win-win situations for themselves and consumers. They created foods and delivery systems that profitably satisfy what consumers want or need. There is no reason to believe that addressing the obesity problem will be different. Having the motivation to profitably address this issue will produce resourceful results, as it has for many other win-win situations in the past.

It's important to realize that a person doesn't become obese overnight. Eighty percent of the population gains weight because of a calorie excess of less than fifty calories a day; fifty extra calories a day can become a big problem over the long term. Gradual problems seldom have instant solutions. Regardless of how ingenious a solution is, it is not likely to be a quick fix. However, simple steps can be taken to help turn back the tide a few calories at a time.

After examining three principles of human behavior that lead us to this problem, this chapter outlines the five main drivers of food consumption. I examine each in terms of what smart marketers and motivated companies can do to counter the effect of this driver in a responsible manner.

Three Principles of Human Behavior That Cannot Be Changed

A number of contributing factors have made us a more obese culture than we were a century ago: automobiles, computers, cable TV, video games, remote controls, the Internet, and omnipresent convenience stores have all contributed to our lack of energy output. In addition, food-related companies have made it easier and more efficient for us to do our "hunting and gathering," and they have contributed to greater energy (calorie) input.

Companies have followed three key principles related to our modern-day hunting and gathering efforts: Consumers seek convenience, consumers seek variety, and consumers seek (the option of) value. To deny that these tendencies exist is a mistake for both marketers and public policy officials.

Consumers Seek Convenience

Innovations throughout time have generally involved reducing the amount of effort it took to move (the wheel), to learn (the printing press), or to communicate (the telephone). This is why new houses have ice makers, dishwashers, and attached garages with garage door openers. It also explains why people often prefer driving to walking or biking. When people do prefer to walk (as in New York City) or bike (as in Amsterdam), it is because it is easier or less effortful than the alternatives.

This desire to follow the path of least effort results in a number of changes to our food distribution system that are market driven but also make the environment fat-friendly. Therefore, we get convenient packaging that is easy to open, a wide availability of vending machines, and fast-food restaurants on convenient corners. We get the chance to buy foods instead of having to prepare them.

Consumers Seek Variety and Choice

In response to our desire for variety, we get brand extensions and new flavors. This desire for variety motivates new product innovations that include healthful alternatives that we can choose to adopt or to avoid. Some of these alternatives evolve into products that are well accepted and embraced, such as Diet Coke. Others, such as McDonald's ill-fated McLean sandwich or Hershey's Taste Sensations, are not embraced regardless of their more healthful twist.

In still other cases, healthful variety may be offered but ignored by most. Even if we look across all foods ordered in restaurants, burgers, French fries, pizza, and Mexican food make up almost 50 percent of all food purchases for both men and women (Figure 7.1). By comparison, vegetables and side salads make up only 14 percent of these purchases (NPD Group 2003). Burger King offers a $1 side salad that costs less than medium fries. Despite the healthful alternative, fries out sell salads by thirty to one. It is the large number of burger alternatives and dessert innovations that keep people coming back for more.

Consumers Seek (the Option of) Value

With millions of purchases every day, people usually choose quantity over quality. This is one reason why Wal-Mart is more popular than Macy's. Everyone knows which store sells higher-quality merchandise, but many define value in a way that influences where they shop. Furthermore, although they might not always prefer the less expensive option, they still want it to exist.

The food-related company that provides the most value—the most quantity and quality for the dollar—is rewarded with patronage and repurchase behavior among people who prefer it over its competitors. Whether in the grocery store or in the restaurant, buying combination meals (a burger, French fries, and a soda) often is much less expensive than buying

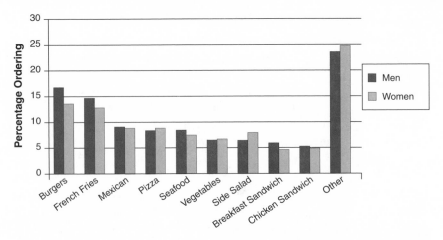

Figure 7.1. Foods most frequently ordered from a restaurant by men and women (NPD Group 2003).

the three items separately. Although a food company might be able to encourage people to eat less by making its food more expensive (either by raising prices or by decreasing portion sizes), forcing them to do so would be foolish. It would disproportionately penalize lower-income consumers, and unless all firms did this, it would result in consumers walking across the street to a competitor.

It is important to realize that these three principles—convenience, variety, and value—drive our hunting and gathering behavior. This knowledge can help us choose realistic marketing strategies that can help to profitably de-market obesity.

Mindful Eating, Moderation, and Exercise

If there is a general theme that should be promoted to address the obesity problem, it is that of mindful eating. Many consumers' eating habits have become routine, scripted, and mindless. Because of the effortlessness of eating, it is easy to misdirect our attention to television, the newspaper, or even our commute while we eat. Not being mindful of what and how much one eats results in overconsumption. Easy fixes, such as labeling, have been proposed to address the obesity problem, but they fail to account for the fact that many consumers are not in situations or mindsets in which they will study a package or nutrition label. Because eating can be a mindless activity, the label is likely to be ignored or viewed as irrelevant to other more interesting distractions.

More information is good, but it is often ignored because using it entails a degree of cognitive control and self-discipline that is impossible for some and very difficult for most. Even if they read a label, some people are unwilling to modify their behavior regardless of what the label says. The role of willpower is of significant concern when it comes to mindful eating.

When food-related companies were confronted with their role in the obesity problem, their initial response was to encourage more moderate eating combined with exercise. Efforts are being made to launch a "Move More, Eat Less" campaign, which is analogous to a pilot study program called "Eat Smart, Play Hard." One concern is finding the right combination of words that resonate with most people. The "eat less" notion may be less effective though, than wording such as "eat reasonably." Such programs certainly will work for some, but not for the entire population.

Many people would lose weight and change their living habits if it were easy to do so. Yet the necessary effort is greater than what many believe is realistic. They think the sacrifice of time, effort, and enjoyment is too costly compared with the alternative. A recent study led by James O. Hall underscores how difficult this "Move More, Eat Less" suggestion is for many: Middle-aged men who had recently suffered a serious heart attack were asked whether they were going to change their eating and exercise habits. A majority of them said they wouldn't consider changing their habits unless they had a second heart attack.

Eating in moderation and exercising more are positive steps, but they will not give overnight results. Just as weight gain is a slow process for most, so is weight loss. This is particularly true when more mild or moderate modifications to behavior are made, such as those suggested by "Move More, Eat Less." Such efforts must be sustained patiently, and our expectations must be modest.

How Companies Can Help Reverse the Drivers of Obesity

Companies can reinforce efforts that encourage people to move more and eat less, and they are also in a position to think more broadly about other ways in which they can help reverse the obesity epidemic among those who are interested in altering their consumption patterns. Recall that consumers tend to seek foods that are convenient, highly varied, and of good value. Given this, what can be done in the short run to combat obesity?

Much of the attention given to what companies can do to help reduce the obesity problem centers around changing packaging or portion sizes or using labels to underscore how much fat is in a product. These are easy targets, but they may not be the biggest threats.

What influences the quantity of food a person consumes? Generally speaking, people eat greater quantities of the foods that are available, easy (inexpensive) to obtain, palatable, safe, and convenient to consume. Each of these drivers of consumption volume can be addressed by sharp, nutrition-conscious marketers or even by consumers themselves (Table 7.1).

Increase the Availability of More Healthful Alternatives

Clearly, if food is not available, it cannot be eaten. A basic finding in this area is that the more effort that is needed to obtain or prepare food, the less of the food people will eat. As effort goes up, consumption goes down. We gave secretaries thirty Hershey's kisses in glass jars and either set the jars on their desks or placed them two meters away from them. Every evening for three weeks we counted how many candies had been eaten and we refilled the jar. We found that secretaries who had jars sitting on their desk ate over twice as many candies each day (9.1 vs. 4.5) as those who had to get up and walk six feet to get them.

The more convenient the food is, the more is eaten. This is why it is not good for a dieter to have extra pints of ice cream or bags of cookies in the house. This is also true in other environments. If people can't find healthful alternatives, they will probably turn to less healthful foods.

One implication for smart marketers is to make healthful options available. Clearly, doing so would benefit the consumers who try these more healthful options, but it would also benefit the company. First, it enables marketers to increase the options offered to consumers and to find successful alternatives that they would not have otherwise investigated. Companies can become functionally fixated on the type of business they are in (e.g., the candy business or the breakfast cereal business). Having to think of expanding or offering alternative or complementary products that are more healthful may help them diversify and develop product lines that they might not have otherwise considered. Second, offering more healthful options can be profitable. These products can be priced competitively or even at a premium. A premium-priced healthful product would be better than no healthful products at all.

Table 7.1. Five Key Drivers of Food Consumption

Consumption Drivers and Recommendations	Relevant Research Findings	*Some* Implications for Responsible Marketers
1. Availability (increase the availability of healthy alternatives)	• The more work or effort it is to get food, the less people eat • Rough rule-of-thumb: Availability → Familiarity → Consumption Frequency	• If people can't find healthy alternatives (say, in a vending machine), they will probably turn to less healthy alternatives. • Help make some healthier alternatives available
2. Cost (increase the cost of consumption but not the cost of food)	• Generally, when prices go up, consumption goes down (except for snack foods) • Warning! There are mixed findings for indulgent foods because of similarly priced alternatives	• Increasing a food's price increases the likelihood that people look for other options. • Increasing knowledge of the types of options available.
3. Palatability (modify food formulations while maintaining palatability)	• People eat what they like • Palatability improves with exposure (recall wine, coffee, and broccoli) • Culture and even labeling can influence perceptions of palatability	• Labeling influences taste • "Diet" and "low calorie" labels influence post-trial taste perceptions, sometimes positively, sometimes negatively. • Test how labeling influences how people *think* a product tastes.
4. Knowledge (provide understandable labels but be realistic)	• Knowledge influences consumption in extreme cases of risk (BSE and spoiled food) • There is no compelling evidence that information and labels influence consumption volume. • There is a confirmatory information bias (we read and believe what confirms what we want to believe and do)	• Labels are good, but they have less influence on consumption than we think. • Labeling works with some people in some situations • Works best when big differences exist between perception and reality
5. Convenience (alter convenience by altering package size and portions)	• People eat what and *as much* as they think is acceptable of a convenient food • Packages, portion sizes, and "meal deals" implicitly suggest what is an appropriate size or combination of food	• Reduced sizes will either (1) reduce consumption among current consumers, or (2) cause these consumers to eat a competitor's food • Consider multipacks with smaller individual servings • Consider premium priced smaller packaging

The reasoning behind this concept is not altogether new. Companies have tried to provide more healthful alternatives in the past (primarily through segmentation efforts). Some, such as diet soda, were tremendously successful. Others, such as the McDonald's McLean sandwich, were not. A multi–million-dollar research and development effort finally resulted in Hershey's being able to manufacture a low-fat chocolate, which was almost identical (from a sensory aspect) to regular chocolate. The product, Sweet Inspirations, was a disappointing market failure. If customers could not have all of the indulgence, they wanted none of the calories. Because Sweet Inspirations was perceived as being halfway between, it failed.

Market success is one benchmark of a new product's viability. Yet when facing some of the threats of the obesity issue, simply having more nutritious alternatives available might be a successful strategy. Consider the "caffeine crisis" of the early 1990s. The allegation was that major soft drink manufacturers, such as Coke and Pepsi, were loading their soft drinks with caffeine to make them more addictive. Rather than attempt to address the merit of these allegations with studies, disclaimers, or experts, both companies simply defused the issue by launching noncaffeinated versions of their products. Although both companies still sell noncaffeinated versions of their regular and diet colas, they are less popular than the caffeinated versions. However, it still makes sense to keep them on the market. As long as they are available, the companies will not have to address the issue of caffeine. In effect, the existence of the product preempts allegations that may be difficult to address.

Many efforts to address the obesity problem may be of a similar nature. It may be that simply providing a wider range of options to consumers will satisfy the concern that there are insufficient healthful options. Although this, in itself, may have only a small effect, it could be significant in combination with other efforts that will be discussed.

Increase the Cost of Consumption but Not the Cost of Food

Generally, when prices go up, consumption goes down. Although this is true in basic macroeconomics, things can change a bit in the micro-economic world of consumption. If the prices of utilitarian foods such as meat and potatoes increase, their consumption decreases. With the more hedonic foods, it is not clear that small changes in prices lead to decreased consumption. A small number of studies have shown that increasing the price of selected vending machine candies caused people to buy less. What is not clear, however, is whether these people simply chose another type of candy. This is typically what has been found with fast food restaurants. Increases in prices at Restaurant X lead to decreases in the incidence of consumption at Restaurant X. However, this does not mean that people are eating salads and broccoli instead of hamburgers. Instead, it probably means that people are opting for a competing fast food restaurant (Restaurant Y).

What is certain is that large increases in food prices also increase the likelihood that people will look for other options. It does not mean that they look for more healthful options. It does not change their wants and food desires; it just changes where they buy their French fries and candy bars.

One solution is to redesign packages so they help people more naturally govern how much they eat. Reducing package sizes would reduce consumption, but it would also make consumers believe they were not getting the value they desire, and this could lead them to defect to a competitor. One solution to this would be to offer smaller packages along with the normal packages and to charge a higher per unit price for them. In this way, both groups would be happy. Those who wanted to remain with the larger (lower unit cost) package would be able to do so, and those who wanted to pay extra in order to combat their lack of self-control could buy the smaller package.

A number of other package-related changes could also be made along these lines. One problem with eating a large package of a product is that consumption is a continuous process wherein we continue to eat until we decide to stop. Because our gastrointestinal system does not immediately signal that it is full, we can continue to eat long after we have eaten enough to fill us. Unless we are eating slowly, or unless someone interrupts our consumption, we may eat more than we should. Once we begin to eat, we can mindlessly continue until we decide it is time to stop or until we reach a natural stopping point.

One way to interrupt this process is to create a natural stopping point. This can be done by separating a large container into several smaller containers. It can also be done through the use of internal sleeves that cause a person to actively decide whether he or she wants to continue with their consumption past the point of finishing one sleeve.

Modify Food Formulations While Maintaining Palatability

People eat what they like. For some products, however, palatability improves with exposure (recall your first experience with wine, coffee, or broccoli). In other cases, culture and even labeling can influence one's perception of a food's taste. For instance, it has been found that words such as "diet" and "low calorie" on labels influence posttrial taste perceptions, sometimes positively, sometimes negatively. In general, it is important to test any effort to change the labels on a product. It is not always how a product tastes that is important; as emphasized in chapter 3, it is also important how people think it will taste.

Although palatability influences *whether* a food is eaten, it only partly influences *how much* is eaten. If a food tastes good, part of what influences how much is eaten is simply how much is usually eaten. As research by Dr. Barbara Rolls has indicated, people become accustomed to consuming a certain volume of food during a day, yet the volume they consume is typically independent of the calorie density of the food. To put this differently, if a person is accustomed to eating four platefuls of food in a typical day, the calorie content of those plates can vary quite a bit without a person realizing that he or she is eating different amounts of calories.

One way to influence how much people eat is to modify the formulation of the foods they eat. If part of the fat in a food is replaced with water, fiber filler, or even air, it would appear to have the same volume, but its calorie density would be lower. Research regarding slightly modified and reformulated foods suggests three key conclusions: When the calorie density of a food is unknowingly decreased, people eat the same volume that they would usually eat; they rate themselves as being as satisfied as those who ate the more calorie-dense foods; and they do not perceive the foods as tasting worse as long as they have not been labeled as being lower in calories. Indeed, sensory tests show that consumers cannot detect small to moderate changes in a food's taste if the calorie density is reduced through the use of water, air, or vegetables.

The failure of a myriad of low-fat products, such as the McLean sandwich, seemingly but erroneously points at the folly of low-calorie foods. What must be realized is that these foods typically were new products that tasted new, were advertised as new, and were expected (by consumers) to be new. Another approach would be to quietly alter existing products in modest ways that reduce calorie density. In this way, no potentially negative expectations of a healthful food are raised that could cause people to believe they will dislike the product before they taste it.

Small modifications in formulations can reduce calorie intake without actually reducing the size of a product. High–energy density ingredients, such as those that are high in fat, can be replaced with low-density ingredients (such as protein or fruits and vegetables).

Size is one of the biggest drivers of how consumers perceive value: the bigger the food, the better the perceived value. Adding water, air, or filler may do little to the taste, but it helps maintain the perception of value and decreases calorie levels. Even if such efforts reduce calorie levels by only 10 percent, a 10 percent decrease in one's daily calorie consumption would reverse weight gain in 90 percent of the population. Prices could be correspondingly altered depending on who was being targeted with the information. It is important to remember that this would occur slowly, however.

Provide Understandable Labels but Be Realistic

For many years, one of the big drivers in how much people consumed was the information they had about whether a food was safe to eat. Sweet berries probably were safe to eat, and sour ones weren't. Good-smelling meat could be eaten; bad-smelling meat couldn't. The food information we receive now comes in different forms. In many people's eyes the information we get from labels is a lot less critical to our health and safety. The products typically have already been approved by the Food and Drug Administration, inspectors, or the grocer. Because other vigilant parties use their eyes, ears, and noses to serve as our food scouts, we don't have to.

In general, most people have a strong confirmatory bias when they seek information. They read and hear what confirms what they want to believe and supports what they want to do. Although accurate calorie and ingredient labeling is uncontroversial, it has much less influence on consumption than we think. Many people do not appear to be eager to learn the details about the foods they eat. Even when they do know the details, they do not always change their behavior.

To date, there is no compelling evidence that information and labels influence consumption volume. Yet we have reason to believe that labels might work with some people under some circumstances. If knowledge provides fat-fighting power for a reasonable size segment, it might be worth the negative or misleading tradeoffs it can have for other segments.

There is a tremendous bias toward believing that if we provide perfect information, people will respond in a perfectly predictable way. But although people know that it is good to do sit-ups and bad to eat potato chips, many will forgo the sit-ups but not the chips.

Yet the notion that nutrition knowledge is power is a bias shared by many regulatory agencies and consumer groups. It's appealing. It assumes that food choices are made by mindful, rational individuals. In reality, most consumers have many more things to think about than what they are eating: their families, their work, and so on. Consumers simply have too many things to think about to mindfully process all nutrition information that is presented to them.

Compare Subway with McDonald's. Subway is heralded as fighting obesity by having low-calorie substitutes and by having nutrition information (for some low-calorie sandwiches) on every napkin, every glass, and every table tent. This should make them the model of healthful eating. In contrast, McDonald's is widely criticized for misleading the public about the nutritional content of their food and its health consequences. If knowledge is power, all the information offered at Subway should make people better informed and healthier consumers.

In a recent study we intercepted diners as they left Subway and McDonald's. They were asked a number of nutrition-related questions, were asked what they ate, and were asked to estimate how many calories they had consumed. Despite the abundant nutrition information at Subway, only 14 percent of those who dined there less than a minute earlier could recall any of this information. Furthermore, although they ate fewer calories than McDonald's patrons, they believed they ate a great deal less than they actually ate. Despite the presence of label information, they did not use it, and the "health cue" it provided caused people to believe an Italian sub with extra mayonnaise and chips was a nutritious choice.

Could label information be effective? Label information might be most effective if it focuses on the consequences of eating a product ("you'll lose weight") instead of simply the characteristics or attributes of the product itself ("this has 200 calories"). There is emerging evidence that labels focused on the consequences of eating ("this bag is the equivalent to 0.05 pounds or the equivalent of walking ten miles") tend to be more effective than those focused on attributes such as calories. Although it is important to provide information, we must be realistic about the minimal effect it will have on most people and on the negligible effect on most of the rest.

nience by Altering Package Size and Portions

>d companies always seem to super-size? There are two reasons:
onsumer demand for value and to match the competition. If a
nber of people want to receive a large meal for their money, the
ny that provides the super-sized meals will be the first company
ipture these consumers. If competitors do not follow suit, they will
ose customers.

Package sizes and shapes influence how much one consumes. The size of a package can implicitly suggest the appropriate amount to eat. In fact, it's believed that they subtly do so regardless of our experience and regardless of whether we like the product. People eat as much as they think is acceptable. Packages, and the portion sizes they suggest, have a significant impact on how much people think they should eat.

A comprehensive set of studies in the 1990s examined how different size packages of forty-eight different products influenced how much people poured (Wansink 1996). In a wide variety of situations, people were asked to pour various amounts, such as how much spaghetti sauce they would pour if making a dinner for two or how much oil they would use if frying chicken for two. Some people were given small packages and others were given packages twice as large. In all cases (except one involving bleach), people poured 15 to 48 percent more from the larger packages. There were some interesting differences depending on the type of product category. If the product was a utilitarian or more healthful product (spaghetti sauce), they would pour about 18 percent more, but if the product was hedonic or less healthful (chocolate), consumption almost doubled.

One reason for this is that people perceived the products to be less expensive per unit (which they were). This also occurs because consumption is more of an automatic process with many people. That is, regardless of whether a product is preferred or even tastes good, people automatically eat more because the serving size suggests how much they should eat.

To examine this, we gave moviegoers either large or extra large containers of popcorn. It was found that these moviegoers ate about 45 percent more from the extra large containers than from the slightly smaller containers. This was repeated using stale popcorn that was fourteen days old, and similar results were found. Even though people disliked the stale popcorn, those with the large containers still ate about 33 percent more on average (Wansink and Park 2001). This attests to the somewhat automatic nature of consumption intake, even when the food tastes bad.

Packages, portion sizes, and "meal deals" imply an appropriate size or combination of food. Reducing these sizes may cause consumers to reduce their consumption of the food, but it is more likely that they will simply eat the larger sizes of a competitor's food because it is a better value.

Perhaps a more subtle but potentially profitable approach would be to manufacture multipacks of products with smaller individual servings. For instance, instead of one twenty-ounce bag of potato chips, one could offer a large bag containing four five-ounce sleeves. This would provide a natural break point at which a person could stop eating.

Another option would be to manufacture smaller, premium-priced packages. Although they would not be priced competitively (per unit) with larger packages, they would satisfy the person who was willing to sacrifice value in order to counter a lack of willpower.

Lessons for Marketing Nutrition

For thousands of years, people have sought tasty foods that they can have in large quantities at their convenience. This is exactly what food companies have given us. Is there any way food companies can also help us choose more wisely? It's important to realize that a person doesn't become obese overnight. Eighty percent of the population gains weight because of an excess of less than fifty calories a day. Gradual problems seldom have instant solutions. Regardless of how ingenious a solution is, it is not likely to be a quick fix. However, there are reasonable steps we can take to help turn back the tide a few calories at a time.

Certainly, we can encourage people to exercise and eat in moderation (in terms of both frequency and quantity). Some companies provide or sponsor exercise or fitness areas in their communities to make it easier for people to become more active. Although both are excellent steps in the right direction, they may be more effective if combined with efforts that directly influence the choices offered to consumers. While examining the features that are most responsible for driving food consumption (availability, cost, effort, palatability, information, and convenience), I make five suggestions that will benefit both companies and consumers. These involve increasing the availability of alternatives, increasing the cost of consumption but not the cost of food, modifying food formulations while maintaining palatability, providing understandable labels, and altering convenience by altering package size and portions.

Should these changes been made quietly or with fanfare? If calling attention to these efforts would alert consumers to issues that were previously of no interest to them, they should not be promoted. In contrast, if promoting them would deflect criticism or if a company wants to establish itself as a responsible industry leader, they should be promoted. It is important to not promise more than one can achieve. It is unlikely that such changes will reverse the obesity problem quickly. However, they will slow it down and eventually promote weight loss. The concern is that if too much is promised and immediate effects aren't seen, the results would be disappointing, and public reactions might backfire.

At this point in our history, the greatest improvements in our life span and quality of life are likely to come more from behavioral changes—eating right and exercising more— than from new medicines. Smart, well-intentioned marketers may be best suited to promoting such changes. Eating habits are a good place to start.

EIGHT

Why Five-a-Day Programs Often Fail

"Eat five servings of fruits and vegetables a day." Much research has been done on why some consumers follow this food guideline while others agree it is a good idea and then eat potato chips. Although much effort and money have been invested in programs such as the "Five-a-Day" program, there is no evidence that these programs are cost-effective, and many doubt whether they are working at all. Some findings, such as those in Figure 8.1, show that consumers are claiming to eat fewer fruits and vegetables as time goes on. This figure indicates a steady and embarrassing decline over the course of the "Five-a-Day" program.

An overriding theme of this book has been the importance of segmenting consumers and viewing them differently based on their beliefs, behaviors, or preferences. In this way, communication efforts, such as encouraging people to eat more fruits or vegetables, can be more effectively tailored. In marketing nutrition, it is not enough to examine why people eat fruits and vegetables; it is important to understand why some people eat fruits instead of vegetables and vice versa.

People who frequently consume fruits or vegetables typically are treated as a homogeneous group by researchers and health care professionals attempting to modify consumption. However, it is widely known that education, region, race, age, and income levels have significant influences on fruit and vegetable intake. It is less clear what causes different preferences for fruits and vegetables. Although Drewnowski (2000) has shown growing evidence of a genetic explanation, there may also be behavioral traits

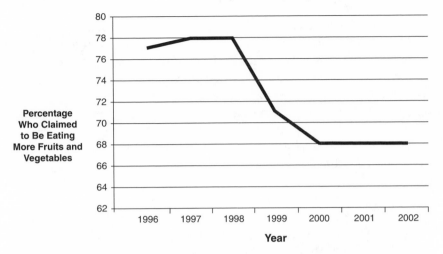

Figure 8.1. Is the "Five-a-Day" program really working? (Food Marketing Institute 2002.)

that distinguish people with strong taste preferences for vegetables from those with strong taste preferences for fruit. Understanding behavioral differences between fruit and vegetable lovers has important implications for researchers and health care professionals.

A growing body of work is finding psychosocial and behavioral traits that are useful in differentiating food preferences. This chapter explores whether behavior-related factors can distinguish fruit lovers from vegetable lovers. After identifying eating behaviors and cooking behaviors that might distinguish fruit lovers from vegetable lovers, we administered a survey of 770 North Americans. The results can be used to more carefully target educational messages, thereby increasing consumption and decreasing health risks.

The purpose of this chapter is not to explain the causal link between behavior and preferences, nor is it to exhaustively identify all potential differences between fruit and vegetable lovers. The true purpose is to identify potentially important discriminators and to emphasize that accounting for such predispositions will make clinical research more precise and thereby make educational and outreach activities more effective.

Why Fruit Lovers and Vegetable Lovers Are Different

Because the culinary uses, tastes, and even health-related effects of fruits and vegetables vary widely, it is reasonable to examine them separately.

For instance, whereas fruits typically are sweet, vegetables have diverse flavors and often are described as bitter or savory. Because fruits generally are sweeter than vegetables, it may be that fruit lovers prefer sweeter foods or have a greater preference for desserts than vegetable lovers. Similarly, vegetable lovers may have a greater preference for savory or spicy foods.

Fruits typically are eaten raw and consumed most often for breakfast, lunch, or between-meal snacks. Fruits can be eaten at the table or on the run. Therefore, they are an ideal breakfast food. If this is true, busy people who take the time to eat breakfast may be more likely to be fruit lovers than vegetable lovers.

Conversely, vegetables are more often cooked with meals or are supplemented with other flavors, sauces, or dressings. Even when eaten raw, many vegetables must be peeled or otherwise prepared. Because eating vegetables often entails more involvement, people who like vegetables might also be more accustomed to food preparation. In fact, it has been anecdotally reported that good cooks can be differentiated by the extent to which they use vegetables in their recipes (recall chapter 6). This tendency has also been related to the extent to which they try new recipes.

It is important to note that not all fruit lovers and not all vegetable lovers are the same. That is, there are subsegments of fruit lovers who are gourmet chefs, and there are subsegments of vegetable lovers who often eat desserts. The purpose of this discussion is to suggest some general similarities that may define these two groups. Based on this general discussion, it would be reasonable to examine whether, in general, vegetable lovers cook more often and more creatively than fruit lovers. Furthermore, it would be reasonable to determine whether fruit lovers ate desserts and breakfasts more often than vegetable lovers. The purpose of this chapter is to examine empirical generalizations that account for heterogeneity and see whether fruit lovers and vegetable lovers are different.

From Supermarkets to Surveys

To begin building the survey instrument, we conducted interviews with fruit lovers and vegetable lovers to determine whether the previously mentioned areas of eating and cooking behavior would be worth exploring. In two supermarket locations in Illinois and Michigan, thirty-seven shoppers (63 percent female, average age thirty-six) who were buying unusually large amount of fruits or vegetables were interviewed for an average of twelve minutes. These semistructured interviews focused on issues related to eating and cooking behavior and enabled us to explore potential distinctions between fruit and vegetable eaters that prior research had not suggested.

The survey instrument was based on a literature review and these interviews. First, we asked questions that enabled us to distinguish between fruit lovers and vegetable lovers. Next, we asked standard frequency questions related to eating and cooking behaviors in the form of "typicality questions" (e.g., "In the typical month, how many times have you had guests for dinner?"). Two thousand people were chosen randomly from census data in fifty states; 770 complete surveys were returned.

Vegetable Lovers versus Fruit Lovers

The results show that there are differences in cooking and eating habits that distinguish fruit lovers from vegetable lovers. As seen in Figure 8.2, vegetable lovers tended to eat spicy food more often, whereas fruit lovers tended to eat desserts more often. The results are consistent with what one might expect. That is, because fruit generally has a higher sugar content than vegetables, fruit lovers may have more of a sweet tooth, and this might be evidenced in more frequent dessert consumption. Similarly, vegetable lovers might be expected to eat savory, spicy foods more often.

Furthermore, these findings show that, on average, cooking behaviors may also differentiate fruit and vegetable lovers. Vegetable lovers tend to

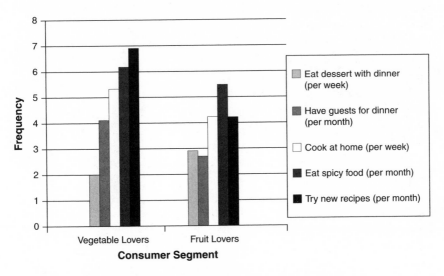

Figure 8.2. Cooking and eating habits of vegetable and fruit lovers.

entertain guests more often, they claimed to cook at home more often, and they claimed to try new recipes more often. These differences are consistent with the observations of Daria (1993) who noted that good cooks tend to have an appreciation and a talent for working with vegetables.

Although this does not explain a person's preference for fruits or vegetables, it does highlight the fact that there are certain characteristics unique to each group. For years, the two groups have been treated as one large, undifferentiated mass. The differences between these two groups add unwanted noise to clinical or sensory studies if they are not accounted for. These results suggest that a more targeted approach in recognizing these different groups will allow more effective communication strategies. The next section examines one of these groups—fruit lovers—in more detail.

Investigating the Sweet Tooth of the Fruit Lover

Fruit consumption is widely encouraged because it is believed to help reduce the risk of heart disease and various forms of cancer. One general approach to promoting consumption is to identify characteristics of infrequent consumers of fruit, develop educational campaigns that target these people, and analyze the effectiveness of these programs. Much less attention has been paid to *frequent* consumers of fruit. Although some efforts have been made to characterize frequent fruit consumers on the basis of demographics and attitudes, little is known about the other types of foods that they might prefer. Knowing this would enable us to tailor educational and promotional efforts to better encourage fruit consumption among predisposed individuals.

People consistently report that taste—sweetness in particular—is an important factor in influencing fruit selection and consumption. Because sweetness contributes to the taste appeal of fruit, it may be that people who like fruits are more attracted to sweet foods in general. That is, people who often eat fruits may also eat sweet snacks more often than other types of snacks, such as salty or savory ones.

Should such a link exist, we would better understand who might be more receptive to nutritional education and promotional efforts for foods. Furthermore, it would also show what food substitutions would have to occur before such people could increase their consumption without increasing their calorie intake.

12,000 Snacking Families Can't Be Wrong

To examine whether fruit consumption is related to sweet snack consumption, we obtained data from the Continuing Survey of Food Intakes by Individuals (CSGII) and the Diet and Health Knowledge Survey (DHKS), taken in 1994–1996. The CSGII consisted of twenty-four–hour dietary recall and demographic information obtained by trained interviewers from a national sample of 12,565 American households. The DHKS was conducted as a randomized telephone follow-up to the CSFII. Questions on this survey related to consumer behavior and attitudes toward diet.

Based on these results, each respondent was placed into one of three groups based on his or her average daily consumption level of fruit: less than one serving, one to two servings, and two or more servings. As expected, frequent fruit consumption was associated with frequent consumption of sweet snacks (Figure 8.3).

Fruit Lovers Eat More Sweet Snacks but Not More Salty Snacks

This higher level of daily fruit consumption was associated with higher levels of sweet snack consumption for both the first day of the survey and the second. This increase in daily fruit consumption had no corresponding effect on salty snack consumption for the first day of the survey. On the

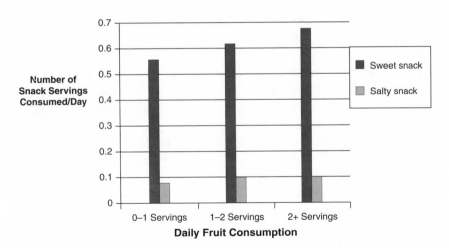

Figure 8.3. Correlation of fruit consumption with sweet and salty snack consumption.

second day of the survey, salty snack consumption increased for those who had one serving of fruit but increased no further for those who had two or more servings.

The absence of a reliable relationship between fruit consumption and salty snack consumption was also found in the DHKS survey. In specifically examining potato chips and corn chips (which are the most common salty snacks), the consumption of chips was constant across the three levels of fruit consumers. As Figure 8.3 indicates, these results from the CSGII survey and the DHKS combine to indicate that frequent consumers of fruit tend to prefer sweet over savory snacks.

It might appear that this fruit–sweet snack relationship exists because people who eat large quantities of food will do so regardless of whether they are eating fruit or snacks. This was not the case. People who were frequent consumers of fruit were also frequent consumers of sweet snacks, but they were not frequent consumers of salty snacks.

Lessons for Marketing Nutrition

Although this chapter does not attempt to explain why a particular person prefers fruits or vegetables, it highlights the fact that certain characteristics are typical of fruit lovers and others are typical of vegetable lovers. For years, the two groups have been treated as one large, homogeneous group. From a research perspective, the heterogeneity between these two groups adds unwanted noise to clinical or sensory studies if it is not properly accounted for in the analysis.

From a marketing perspective, educational or promotional efforts (such as the "Five-a-Day" program) that treat fruit and vegetable lovers as homogeneous may be less effective than ones that treat fruit lovers differently from vegetable lovers.

It is important not to assume that all fruit lovers behave in one way and all vegetable lovers in another. Yet our findings generally indicate that there are important differences in preferences that must be identified and taken into account when studying the response of different populations to clinical research treatments or education programs. Researchers can do so by asking questions about fruit or vegetable consumption when prescreening subjects, or these data can be used as covariates in assessing the impact of different treatments or clinical trials. For health professionals and educators, the importance of targeting different messages to differently predisposed publics can mean the difference between effective programming and wasted effort.

These findings suggest that when one is studying the consumption frequency of one food, it is also important to understand the consumption frequency of related foods. By recognizing taste preferences, we can better determine why fruit lovers tend to eat sweet snacks, for example. This, in turn, can help us better understand what drives the consumption frequency of various foods. For instance, when we try to identify those who are most likely to increase their fruit consumption, we should consider people who frequently eat sweet snacks. These people are more likely to have a taste profile that mirrors that of frequent fruit consumers than those who instead prefer salty snacks.

Indeed, to increase the effectiveness of programs such as the "Five-a-Day" campaign, we can develop taste profiles for frequent consumers of both fruits and vegetables. Such information could enable more effective targeting and message strategies. One suggestion for nutrition education programs is to analyze marketing strategies of sweet snacks (such as candy bars) and incorporate these techniques into an intervention program that instead attempts to increase fruit consumption.

NINE

Winning the Biotechnology Battle

Functional foods and biotechnology often are wrongly perceived as interconnected in many consumers' minds. New foods, enhanced with added nutritional characteristics, can be intimidating. Some consumers are afraid to try functional foods such as soy, fermented dairy products, and yogurt because they have preconceived notions about the risks involved with adopting them. Some consumers refuse to adopt new foods based on emotion, fear, or unfounded beliefs.

How can we reduce such fear? If we look at consumer reactions to biotechnology, we can predict a lot about their behavior. Both proponents and opponents of biotechnology claim that their goal is to educate consumers so they can make more informed decisions. Opponents focus on the risks of biotechnology, and proponents focus on the benefits. Yet neither side has generated strong support, and many consumers are still confused about the issue. This confusion and the ineffectiveness of such education efforts can be partially attributed to inaccurate assumptions both groups make about consumers. Throughout this chapter, we'll see how the riskiness of biotechnology relates to consumers' perceptions of functional foods and foods that have been otherwise genetically enhanced. Biotechnology is the modification of the genetic material of living cells so they will produce new substances or perform new functions. Examples of biotechnologically produced foods include insect-protected potatoes, virus-resistant squash, herbicide-resistant corn, and high–oleic acid soybeans.

This chapter looks at both the proponents and the opponents of biotechnology to see how understanding both groups will help marketers become more effective at educating consumers about functional foods and biotechnological advances. Proponents of biotechnology, particularly biotechnology corporations, base their marketing campaigns on a commodity promotion mindset and on market share advertising. They assume that the biotechnology controversy will soon be forgotten, that science sells and fear fails, that biotechnology education is a trade association concern, and that what's good for medicine is good for food.

Opponents or skeptics of biotechnology, such as environmentalists, base their strategies on grassroots experiences. They assume that consumers want to be informed, that consumers need to be informed, that the risks of the unknown are more important than the benefits, and that changes in consumer attitudes will lead to changes in behavior.

Understanding key principles of consumer psychology will enable both groups to be more effective in educating consumers. This chapter explains how consumers form attitudes toward biotechnology. It then discusses the fallacies in the assumptions of the opponents and proponents. Finally, it provides implications for more effective consumer education that can be applied to increase consumption of functional foods.

How Consumers Form Attitudes toward Biotechnology

Consumers' attitudes toward biotechnology are divided and do not appear to be moving toward consensus. One mail survey asked 1,036 Americans, "What is your opinion toward biotechnology?"; 31 percent favored it, 18 percent opposed it, 26 percent had mixed feelings, and 26 percent did not care or had no opinion (Doyle 2000). Views were sharply divided. Some people liken biotechnology to other forms of progress such as the automobile or computer: "Man has been engineering his environment since day one, so what's the fuss all about?," "I'm all for using less resources to improve yield," "A hundred years from now people will laugh at our superstitions regarding this new technology," "Just as in the past, what's new and improved is often mistaken as harmful."

Others disagree: "The genetics scares the hell out of me. I am in the stage of my life that most of it is behind me, and hopefully the genetics will not affect me, but it sure will (affect) the generations below me." Some consumers focus on the benefits of biotechnology, whereas others focus on the risks. Some study the issue carefully, whereas others view it emotionally. According to consumer psychology, there are two general ways or routes—central and peripheral—through which attitudes are formed (Petty and Cacioppo 1981). When people are motivated to understand an issue and have the ability and opportunity to do so, their attitudes will be formed through a direct, central route. When they are not motivated to understand the issue, when they lack the technical or cognitive ability to understand it, or when they lack the opportunity to think about it, their attitudes will be formed through an indirect or peripheral route.

When attitudes are centrally formed, a consumer's attitude toward biotechnology is determined by beliefs about various aspects of biotechnology, weighted by the importance he or she gives to each belief. Attitude is the sum of all positive and negative beliefs about the target, weighted by their importance. Because beliefs are subjective, they are not always correct and can vary dramatically across consumers. Furthermore, the weights given to specific information or beliefs can vary across people even if they share some common beliefs. These differences can lead two people with very similar experiences and beliefs to have two different attitudes toward biotechnology.

Recent studies have shown that consumers view genetic engineering technology as a risky process for different reasons. Some of them perceive environmental risks (threats to ecological balance and reduced biological diversity), safety risks (lack of control and difficulty in measuring safety), and ethical considerations (discomfort with "playing God" and concerns about the health and welfare of animals). However, if genetically modified products offer important benefits, these benefits may outweigh the perceived risks. Just as there are environmental risks, there are also environmental benefits (reduced use of chemical pesticides and water and soil protection), health benefits (development of medicines and "edible vaccines" along with better nutrition and food quality), and agricultural benefits (protection against diseases, increased productivity, and biodiversity and sustainability).

When consumers have little motivation to process biotechnology information, little ability to understand it, or little time to digest it, their opinions are formed by the peripheral route. Under these circumstances, their focus is not on the claims and arguments made in the message but on nonmessage factors or cues such as public opinion, soundbites, emotions generated by advertising, labeling, or the credibility of spokespeople or endorsers.

That people can be aware of an issue without having specific knowledge of it is well supported. This "high awareness but low knowledge" characterization is common in the biotechnology area because of the newness and complexity of genetic engineering.

Education Fallacies of Biotechnology Opponents

Educating consumers about the benefits and risks of biotechnology, trying new foods, or adopting functional foods requires knowing how consumers learn. By looking at the biotechnology example in more detail, we can generalize key findings and apply them to increase functional food consumption. Both opponents and proponents of biotechnology make assumptions about consumers that limit their effectiveness in communicating with the public. Without hard evidence against the outcomes of biotechnology, opponents have tended to focus on the process. They have used demonstrations and publicity campaigns to target consumers and to lobby government agencies. Their approach has focused on ethical and social issues and the fear caused by uncertainty. These efforts reflect a set of assumptions that opponents of biotechnology make about consumers. To be more effective, they must revise each of these assumptions. If we learn how to effectively educate consumers and address these common assumptions, we can better understand the market and better define a marketing strategy.

Opponent Fallacy 1: People Want to Be Informed

Consumers vary greatly in how much they want to be informed about issues. The most successful daily newspapers in the world penetrate less than 40 percent of the households in their market, and situation comedies generate more television viewers than the average network news broadcast. Whereas some consumers centrally process and actively formulate an informed opinion about biotechnology, others are more willing to trust outside agencies to make biotechnology decisions for them. The first group is called information seekers and the latter group institutionalists.

Most consumers appear to be institutionalists when it comes to food safety issues, believing that decisions about the safety of biotechnology should be left to the experts. Although these experts can be scientists or regulatory agencies, they may also include the moral expertise of religious groups or the perceived ethical expertise of a special interest group. Whatever alternatives are presented to them have been preapproved by these experts. Although one might assume that institutionalists tend to be people with less formal education, even those with advanced education find themselves ill equipped or unwilling to spend time studying the issue. They welcome the involvement of experts who can provide them with the conclusion to the issue and not the details it takes to arrive at that conclusion.

In contrast, some consumers want to know about the details behind the biotechnology issue. When these information-seeking consumers want to learn about the risks and benefits of biotechnology and genetic engineering, they turn first to the media and personal discussions, and then to informational brochures. Other consumers acquire biotechnology information from magazines, government publications, consumer organizations, and research institutes. Knowing where these people go for information is important. Reading newspaper reports of demonstrations and protests is less important and less persuasive to information seekers than reading a more informative view in a magazine or brochure.

Opponent Fallacy 2: People Need to Be Informed

Unlike many other countries, the United States has benefited from a strong food regulatory system for many years. As a result, food safety vigilance is not an important issue, and it is generally entrusted to regulatory organizations. A recent poll indicated that 83 percent of Americans trust the Food and Drug Administration (FDA) (Hadfield, Howse, and Trebilcock 1998). Next to the Supreme Court, it is the most trusted government agency.

For many busy people, second-guessing the food-related decisions of a risk-averse government is not worth their time or effort. Food scares in the United States have been tied to violations of FDA standards or regulations, not to oversights or mistakes in the regulations themselves. Given this track record, many consumers believe there is no reason to distrust or second-guess the regulatory system. Many consumers do not want to be informed largely because they do not believe they need to be informed.

Opponent Fallacy 3: Risks of the Unknown Are More Important

Benefits often are more important than risks to consumers. Consumers become willing to accept biotechnology products when they become convinced that such products offer significant benefits over other products. These benefits can include decreases in price and increases in product quality (taste and naturalness), purity (fewer chemicals), and nutrition. Hamstra's (1995) study of Dutch consumers reported that perceived benefits had a greater statistical influence on attitudes and acceptance than did perceived risks.

Even for opponents of biotechnology, benefits often outweigh risks. Sometimes, however, social benefits are more heavily weighed than personal benefits. Sheehy, Legault, and Ireland (1998) demonstrated that consumers considered genetically engineered potatoes that reduced the need for environmentally harmful pesticides as being significantly more beneficial than those with prolonged shelf life and improved taste.

History has repeatedly shown that many people's principles have a price associated with them. That is, if it costs too much (in terms of money or forgone utility) to uphold the principle, they let it slip. For instance, a principled stand against the radiation emanating from microwaves becomes a nonissue after one receives a microwave oven for a birthday present. An opponent of fur becomes a silent champion after inheriting a coat with fur trim. The "white meat only" advocate secretly enjoys beef when fish becomes too expensive. A philosophical stance against biotechnology has a price, although it is unseen in consumer surveys. Sometimes it is measured as a difference in cost, other times as a difference in convenience. In still others, it fades away as supporters of the cause become weary of the issue.

Opponent Fallacy 4: Changing Consumer Attitudes Will Change Their Behavior

The assumption that negative attitudes toward biotechnology will lead people to not purchase a biotechnology product seems reasonable. Yet attitudes often do not predict behavior. Heijs and Midden (1995) investigated the impact of attitudes on behavioral intentions across four examples of genetically engineered food. Intention to buy each of the foods was used as a measure of positive intention, and intention to protest against the foods was a measure of negative intention. Consumers who valued the benefits of biotechnology indicated that they would purchase the food. In contrast, there was no similar correspondence with the negative intention measure. In essence, there was little relationship between biotechnological attitudes and behavior. This can be attributed to the weak impact of attitudes on behavior once the differences in the cost or convenience of products become noticeable.

Biotechnology can be complex and difficult to understand. When consumers are confused, they sometimes defer their choices until they can develop proper evaluation criteria and acquire enough information.

However, when benefits begin to outweigh risks, behavior may reverse dramatically, and purchases will be made by all but the most extremely opposed consumers. Likewise, as people see more and more biotechnology products under more realistic (nonlaboratory) conditions, they will generally come to accept biotechnology because of its familiarity.

Marketing Fallacies of Biotechnology Proponents

Proponents of biotechnology have their own incorrect assumptions. Their basic strategy has been to focus on the advantages of the technology and on the long-term benefits that are not specific to consumers but are more focused on the global benefits of the products. This strategy suggests a series of misperceptions or fallacies about consumers that limit their communication effectiveness. If we can recognize that these different groups process information differently, we can communicate to each group in a way that reduces the perceived risk associated with biotechnology foods, new foods, or functional foods. By addressing the fallacies described here, we can develop a marketing strategy that best reaches each specific group of people. Furthermore, we can also reduce the inaccurate assumptions about consumers that currently limit the effectiveness of functional food communications.

Proponent Fallacy 1: The Biotechnology Controversy Will Be Forgotten

Opponents of biotechnology generally discuss their opinions with other opponents, and proponents discuss theirs with other proponents. As a result, proponents can underestimate the seriousness of the issue, believing that most people think the way they do. Many firms erroneously think that biotechnology will become less controversial over time.

This belief—or hope—was a critical mistake made by British firms. In 1994, public sentiment toward biotechnology was neutral if not moderately positive. Therefore, the industry made no real efforts to build public support or enthusiasm for biotechnology because attitudes toward it appeared to be improving each month. Even though attitudes were improving, they were still not fully formed or stable. As a result, when mad cow disease became an issue, the industry had not generated an appropriate level of education or a solid enough basis of support to keep the issue in perspective and to keep biotechnology moving forward.

Some proponents in the United States believe that the improving sentiment of the nonvocal majority indicates that the biotechnology controversy will pass. However, they are only one serious episode away from losing all the ground they have gained. Because of the highly sensitive nature of this issue, even a moderately unrelated event could cause the public to overreact. Even if the biotechnology controversy passes, proponents still need to counteract public misperceptions with effective education.

Proponent Fallacy 2: Science Sells and Fear Fails

Consider a person whose attitudes have been formed through the peripheral route to persuasion. With low awareness and knowledge of biotechnology and with no established measures of benefits and risks, his or her attitudes could be easily swayed by peripheral cues such as public opinion, publicity, soundbites, source credibility, labeling, emotion, and fear. To this person, careful scientific reports and expertly articulated third-party testimonials will have little direct impact on his or her attitude toward biotechnology. Indeed, even a judicious FDA endorsement might have less impact than a memorable phrase or the dismal portrayal of genetic engineering in a movie (e.g., *Species, Jurassic Park, Gattaca,* or *DNA*).

One indicator of how peripheral processing dominates attitude formation can be found in the significant role religious and ethical beliefs can play in influencing public concerns about biotechnology applications. Animal rights activists protest biotechnology, arguing that genetically modified animals might suffer vulnerability to specific diseases as the result of such modifications. Some religious groups oppose the use of biotechnology on the ground that experimenting with lives is "playing God." These religious and ethical concerns will become even more vocal as further advances in gene technology bring about fears of human gene selection and cloning. Groups opposing the use of biotechnology on these grounds dictate specific viewpoints to consumers without encouraging objective evaluation. Soundbites such as "playing God" can lead one to peripherally process the issue and to label biotechnology as wrong without considering its benefits.

The fallacy that "science sells" is based on the notion that if consumers are given the facts, they will come to the proper conclusions. Yet even with identical information and beliefs, people will arrive at different conclusions. A well-to-do vegetarian might believe cost savings are less important than caring for animals. A second person might focus more on how biotechnology increases the world food supply and slows land commercialization. A third person might focus on comparing organic gardens of yesteryear with the unknown issues of tomorrow. Attitude formation is further complicated by the fact that consumers not only have different information but also have different values and different ways of combining such information.

Proponent Fallacy 3: Biotechnology Education Is a Trade Association Issue

Biotechnology education is not a trade association issue. The first step of biotechnology education is partly a branding issue. Before people will listen to a proponent's perspective, biotechnology must provide a clear, systematic, vivid, and focused message that is important to consumers. In the biotechnology marketing battle, the opponents of biotechnology clearly have the upper hand. The powerful visuals associated with names such as *Frankenfoods* and *super weeds* can easily sway the public toward skepticism or opposition. These vivid phrases promote peripheral processing instead of a thoughtful consideration of the benefits and risks involved.

Trade associations, scientific organizations, and governments probably cannot brand biotechnology in a way that leaves its benefits clear in a consumer's mind. The majority of trade association efforts in this regard have not been effective. The most notable examples (such as the "Got Milk" campaign) have won awards but reportedly have contributed little to increasing sales among nonusers. If firms are to compete with opponents of biotechnology, they first need to realize that branding biotechnology deserves some of their best marketing minds. It is too important to be outsourced or trusted to a risk-aversive, consensus-building trade association or government agency.

Proponent Fallacy 4: What's Good for Medicine Is Good for Food

Some consumers accept biotechnology for medicinal purposes but not necessarily for foods. These different attitudes toward medicine and food can be explained by the way the situation is framed—or perceived—by consumers. Nobel-prize winning work has shown that people show a risk-taking tendency when the outcome is perceived as the reduction of a loss ("I don't want to be sick"), but they show a risk-aversive tendency when the outcome is perceived as a gain ("I want to be healthy").

In general, biotechnological applications in the medical domain are perceived as loss reductions. For example, the benefit of a new medicine developed with biotechnology generally is seen as improving the lost health of an already ill patient. Thus, it is perceived as a reduction of a loss. However, the benefit of a biotechnological food product is often perceived as only marginally improving nutrition. As such, it is perceived as a modest increase of a gain or benefit.

If the differences in the acceptance of biotechnology across application domains result from differences in how the benefits and risks are perceived or framed, how can opinions be changed? Consumer acceptance of food-related biotechnology may be improved if the benefits are framed in terms of reducing potential dietary hazards instead of enhancing nutrition or quality. As these benefits and losses become more evident, they can be promoted on a food-specific level (e.g., broccoli) or on a category-specific level (e.g., green vegetables). Similarly, an environmental position would take the same approach. Consumer acceptance could be improved if the benefits are framed in terms of reducing destructive pesticides and waste instead of enhancing ecological balance.

Lessons for Marketing Nutrition

The accelerating growth of biotechnology and its applications are interfering with consumer understanding. Even so, a large part of the confusion consumers have about biotechnology can be attributed to misguided communication efforts by proponents and opponents. Both of these groups make inaccurate assumptions about consumers that limit their effectiveness as communicators (Table 9.1). Contrary to what proponents think, the biotechnology controversy will not be forgotten, nor will all people become advocates once they "see the science." Contrary to what opponents think, many people do not care to be informed about the details of biotechnology, and the risks associated with biotechnology will not keep them from enjoying the benefits it can offer.

For both opponents and proponents, continuous education is critical even if it appears that many consumers are not interested in the issue. Although a person might be uninterested in biotechnology today, windows of potential influence often open and close. Continuous education keeps consumers informed and offers uninterested consumers the opportunity to learn. The more effort is invested in education, the less risk there is that consumers will overreact to biotechnology on the basis of emotion, fear, memorable phrases, or unfounded benefits.

In general, both proponents and opponents need to realize that understanding a person's processing style and how it influences attitudes

Table 9.1. Revising Fallacious Assumptions about Consumers and Biotechnology

	Fallacious Assumptions	Accurate Assumptions
Proponents of biotechnology	1. The biotech controversy will be forgotten	1. Continuous biotechnology education is critical
	2. Once people have the facts, they will be bio-tech advocates	2. For the majority of consumers, facts may mean less than memorable phrases
	3. Science sells and fear fails	3. The emotion of biotechnology often wins over reason
	4. Biotechnology education is a trade association issue	4. Biotechnology is a branding and education issue
Opponents of biotechnology	1. People want to be informed	1. Many consumers do not care to be informed
	2. People need to be informed	2. Only active decision makers believe they need to be informed
	3. Changing consumer attitudes will change their behavior	3. Product benefits can cause a person to act differently than their philosophical position would indicate
	4. Risks are more important than benefits	4. Benefits are more important to most people than risks

Source: Wansink and Kim (2001).

is critical. Classifying consumers into several categories based on prior knowledge, information processing style, or current biases toward biotechnology can provide a sound basis for more effective education strategies. This enables messages to be tailored. To illustrate how messages can be tailored, consider three categories of consumers: those with centrally formed attitudes toward biotechnology, those with peripherally formed attitudes, and those with no attitude. Table 9.2 shows how general educational strategies—relevant for both opponents and proponents—would vary across these different attitudes.

Suppose an opponent or proponent of biotechnology wanted to inform consumers with peripherally processed attitudes about newly discovered biotechnology information. The most effective education efforts would use one-sided messages that eliminate misperceptions and are delivered by a biotechnology expert. This is different from how the same information should be directed to a consumer who has no firm attitude

Table 9.2. Attitude Profiles of Consumers and Relevant Education Strategies

How Existing Attitude Was Formed	Relevant Education Strategy
Centrally processed attitude	• Use two-sided message: benefits and risks • Provide reliable statistics • Provide clear evaluation criteria
Peripherally processed attitude	• Consistently reinforce attitude • Focus on eliminating illusions and misperceptions • Consistently reinforce attitude with one-sided message • Use expert endorsers • Keep them abreast of up-to-date information
No attitude	• Use visible and credible endorser • Minimize misleading publicity • Focus education message on basic information • Using publicity and advertising to increase awareness

toward biotechnology. In this case, the message should be focused at a more basic level, perhaps through publicity. If mass media were being used, it would be more effective to use a highly recognizable endorser rather than a credentialed but unknown expert.

Throughout this chapter, I have made no judgment as to who is right. Both opponents and proponents can fairly and effectively educate consumers about the risks and benefits of biotechnology. The more effectively consumers are educated, the more constructive the development of biotechnology will be.

The education strategies suggested here may seem relevant only for large institutions, such as companies or well-organized political action groups. Yet the same basic concept—understanding the processing style of your target audience and how it influences attitudes—is also relevant to individual scientists who want their research to have more impact. University researchers are the most trusted sources of information about biotechnology (Borre 1990), yet their impact is compromised when they misunderstand their audience. Whether researchers are writing, organizing public and professional talks, or answering questions for the media, knowing how consumers make decisions will prevent researchers from making the same mistakes companies and activists have made.

This chapter explored the ramifications of incorrectly assuming how consumers think, emphasizing the need to understand consumers' processing styles and how they influence consumer attitudes. By examining both opponents' and proponents' beliefs about biotechnology products, we gain insight into the consumer thought process. We can conclude that continuous education is critical so that consumers do not simply refuse to adopt new products because of emotion, fear, or unfounded beliefs.

Consumers often react irrationally, based on their emotions or fears. Continuous education about a product, whether it is a biotechnology product or a functional food, minimizes this risk. Ultimately, continuous education promotes consumer acceptance. Before introducing a functional food to the market, it is important to define a target audience and develop a proper segmentation of the market. Consumers may process information differently, but we can still classify these consumers into similar processing styles.

By classifying market segments, we can tailor our marketing message in a way that is most effective in influencing the attitudes of each group. Knowing how consumers make decisions will prevent us from making misguided assumptions about the market and provide the foundation for an effective marketing strategy. By exploring how consumers' attitudes are shaped, we can effectively create a marketing message that best influences the consumers' thought process and ultimately leads to more healthful consumer behavior. In chapter 10, we will explore consumer reactions to a product-related crisis.

Related Reading

This chapter has been adopted from the following article, which provides more detail on the psychology of decision making and the implications for those interested in educating others about biotechnology.

Wansink, Brian. and Junyong Kim. "The Marketing Battle over Genetically Modified Foods: False Assumptions about Consumer Behavior." *American Behavioral Scientist* 44:8 (April 2001): 1405–17.

TEN

Managing Consumer Reactions to Food Crises

Marketing nutrition is a process of encouraging people to make healthful choices that improve their well-being. What happens when contamination, terrorism, or disease is thought to threaten a part of the food supply? Some crises have influenced the recall, redesign, and communication efforts of individual companies (such as Tylenol, Perrier, Ford, Goodyear, and Shell). Others—such as the threat of bovine spongiform encephalopathy (BSE, or mad cow disease) in beef—can compromise an entire industry.

One of the dangers of food safety crises is that they can be triggered by concurrent events. The terrorist attacks of September 11, 2001, in the United States triggered concerns about anthrax attacks. Yet the behavior of consumers in a crisis is not always consistent with the true level of risk they face. This chapter examines how seemingly inconsistent behaviors of consumers can be explained by risk perceptions and risk attitudes. The drivers of consumer behavior provide insights into whether the solution to a crisis lies in more effective communication efforts or in more drastic measures (such as recalls or product eliminations).

Food safety crises dramatically illustrate marketers' need to understand why and how consumers react. Table 10.1 describes six crises that have recently occurred. Although each is slightly different, they all involved a state of panic that could have been prevented if appropriate marketing-related efforts had been made. One reason why many of these food scares

Table 10.1. What Is the Potential Impact of a Food Crisis?

Description	Consumers' Reaction	What Was done	Aftermath
Edwina Currie fiasco (1988, G.B.); junior health minister re-signed after admit-ting most of U.K.'s eggs contaminated with salmonella	Demand for eggs failed; lingering downturn of egg consumption	4 million hens slaughtered; 400 million surplus eggs destroyed	Salmonella poison-ing is permanent problem; 30,000 cases in England & Wales every year
Mad Cow Disease (BSE) in beef by-products for cattle feed (1996, G.B. and E.U.); linked to Creutzfeldt-Jakob disease (CJD) in 1996	Consumption of beef products de-creased; consumers buy more white meat, other meat, organic meat	Beef exports from U.K. to Europe banned; labeling and origin on all meat products	EU ban lifted in 1999; traceability becomes a must
E. coli poisoning (1996, Scotland); 21 people died, 500 ill	It came from a local butcher shop (who had recently won the award for Best Scottish Beef Butcher of the Year)	The butcher was asked to stop sell-ing cooked meat products the next morning after the outbreak was discovered.	Scotland's most seri-ous food poisoning event since 1964; permanent prob-lem everywhere, several cases every year, affecting thousands of people worldwide
Salmonella in dog treats (Canada, October 1999); people may risk bacterial infection by handling the treats directly or by contact with pets who have used the treats	Consumers have to wash their hands and avoid being in contact with the treats	Canadian Food Inspection Agency (CFIA) is warning consumers not to purchase certain dog treats manu-factured by Farm Meats Canada Ltd.	Health Canada planned further studies of natural pet products to ascertain the scope of the problem; several members of the industry took pro-active steps to ensure the safety of their pet treats.
ConAgra Beef (June 2002, U.S.); E. coli in beef products	25 victims total; ConAgra agreed to pay the medical and lost-wage costs of 13 victims in Colorado ($1 mil-lion)	ConAgra recalls 354,000 pounds of beef products; me-dia communicate products' IDs and warn about E. coli	Victims accepted ConAgra's pay-ment of medical expenses, also agreed not to file lawsuits against the company
Listeria in Chicken (2002, U.S.); listeria in Pilgrim's Pride products, 23 deaths, 120 ill	Many people affected in Pennsylvania, New York, New Jersey, Delaware, Maryland, Con-necticut, Ohio, and Michigan renewed push to reform the laws that govern meat inspection	Meat recalled by the company (27 mil-lion pounds); was called by media the "U.S. largest meat recall," but discov-ered afterward that it was exaggerated (2 other events caused larger recalls)	2,500 cases of listerio-sis occur annually in the U.S.

Source: Adapted from Pennings, Wansink, and Meulenberg (2002).

have been so severe is that little thought was given to planning for crises beforehand; another is that people have been expected to respond in a homogeneous manner.

This chapter distinguishes four different segments of consumers who would be most influenced and most influential during a food crisis. Decoupling consumers' risk response behavior into the separate components of risk perception and risk attitude will enable marketers to deal with different segments of consumers in a crisis. The focus will be on precrisis preparations and postcrisis responses.

A Framework for Understanding Public Panic

The study of risk perception has been punctuated by conflict and paradigm shifts. Despite more than three decades of research, our understanding of how consumers assess risk remains fragmented. Until recently, eating food has been viewed as a low-risk activity. Consequently, theories of risk have focused on environmental and technological hazards, such as nuclear power, and have neglected food issues. After a decade of food scares, however, attention has moved toward the study of food risk. Unfortunately, it has focused almost exclusively on the divergence of opinion between experts and the public and has not directly addressed food risk and panic itself.

How consumers respond to food crises is often characterized as a linear process: there's a crisis, there are corporate communications, consumers hear them, and they respond. In reality, consumer response is more sophisticated. Different segments respond differently, and precrisis considerations (such as consumers' previous knowledge and precrisis communication) must be accounted for (Figure 10.1).

At the center of the framework is the notion that there are different segments of consumers who will respond to a food crisis in different ways. Rather than being defined demographically by their education level, ethnicity, or income, they are psychographically defined by whether they have low or high perceptions of risk (e.g., "What is the risk of this beef having BSE?") and by whether they have low or high levels of preexisting risk aversion.

Another important element of this framework is that it differentiates between precrisis preparation and postcrisis response. Efforts in precrisis preparation should be ongoing, and plans for postcrisis communication should be made in advance.

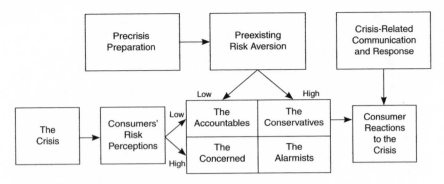

Figure 10.1. Factors influencing consumer responses to a food crisis.

This chapter defines the four segments in the center of the framework and then describes various precrisis preparations and post-crisis responses.

Profiling Consumers to Predict Responses

The risk level of any particular activity (such as getting sick from eating warm potato salad or contracting Creutzfeldt-Jacob disease from eating BSE beef) is perceived differently by different consumers. How consumers cope with perceived risk depends on their risk aversion. People's perceptions of risk and benefit associated with particular foods help determine their acceptance of the food.

As the work of Pennings (2001, 2005) has shown, risk perception is a consumer's interpretation of the likelihood that he or she will be exposed to harm. Risk aversion is a consumer's general predisposition to risk. Some people are very risk averse and others are not; that is one reason why all people in the world do not skydive, ride motorcycles, or hang glide. It is important to emphasize that risk aversion and risk perception are two different concepts. Whereas risk aversion deals with a consumer's interpretation of the nature of the risk and how much he or she wants to avoid it, risk perception deals with the consumer's interpretation of the likelihood of being exposed to harm.

Four Profiles of Consumers

The matrix in Table 10.2 presents four different profiles of consumers, based on their level of risk perception and risk aversion. The higher the risk aversion, the more likely consumers are to refuse any risk under any

Table 10.2. Four Profiles of Consumers According to Risk Perception and Risk Aversion Levels

	Low Risk Aversion	High Risk Aversion
Low Risk Perception	1. The Accountables • "Risk-seeking" consumers • Take the risk to do what they want • Ignore the information	3. The Conservatives • "Risk-averse" consumers • Don't take risks • Seek information, but "silent majority"
High Risk Perception	2. The Concerned • "Risk-averse" consumers • Don't take risks • Their high perception of risk drive their behavior	4. The Alarmists • "Risk-averse" consumers • Don't take risks • Overreact, overinfluence others, politically active

condition; the higher the perception of risk, the less likely consumers are to accept a particular situation. When combined, risk aversion and risk perception allow us to separate consumers into four categories (Wansink 2004a):

The Accountable Segment   The low risk aversion–low risk perception profile corresponds to consumers who are risk seekers. They view themselves as accountable for their own behavior and what results from it. They ignore any available information on risk and keep their habits, even though some risk may be involved in their behavior.

The Concerned Segment   This is the low risk aversion–high risk perception segment. These people have the risk of most behaviors in perspective. They are not risk averse to begin with, so their behavior is dictated primarily by their perception of risk. As their perception of the riskiness of an action increases, they approach a point where they will not participate in the action at all.

The Conservative Segment   This consists of high risk aversion–low risk perception consumers. They are cautious, risk-averse consumers who do not take any unnecessary risks.

The Alarmist Segment   This high risk aversion–high risk perception profile corresponds to risk-averse consumers. They are prone to overreacting to many situations. They are also the most assertive in their tendency to become politically involved or to actively attempt to influence others.

Although seeing the world as roughly consisting of four different profiles of consumers is helpful in predicting responses to a crisis, it is most useful when combined with scenario planning. Scenario planning is one of the most effective methods of planning for military crises, and it provides perhaps the best model for taking precautions and setting up a response plan.

How Can Consumers Respond to a Crisis?

Independent of the scale of the crisis (local, national, or global), a consumer's response can be characterized by different factors that contribute to certain behavioral responses. A large part of predicting consumers' response to a food crisis is examining their risk profile. Consider the four consumer segments just described. Each segment will have a different response to a food crisis. Their responses can be described by three characteristics: the level of aggressiveness (passive vs. aggressive), the level of rationality (irrational vs. rational), and the length of the response (short-term vs. long-term). The behavioral responses for each of the four consumer profiles are described in Table 10.3.

Passive versus Aggressive Responses   When faced with a food crisis, a consumer can respond along a continuum of passive and aggressive responses. A passive response involves simply modifying one's behavior to avoid the danger. In the case of BSE or foot-and-mouth disease, this would simply mean avoiding beef by substituting another product such as chicken or fish.

Consumers can also have a more aggressive response, such as demanding restitution or trying to change the market structure by campaigning for new laws, guidelines, or regulation systems. Both of these responses can critically wound an industry. In Australia, tainted metwurst (a type of sausage) caused several deaths and resulted in a boycott of the entire metwurst industry. Many years after the fact, the industry has not recovered.

Irrational versus Rational Responses   Consumers can respond rationally or irrationally to a food crisis. If the objective facts merit an extreme response (such as not eating the food), then an extreme response is rational. If the objective facts merit a less extreme response (such as fully cooking the food or not eating it raw), than a less extreme response would be considered

Table 10.3. Behavioral Responses to Consumer's Risk Profile

Consumer Segment	Responses		
	Passive vs. Aggressive	Irrational vs. Rational	Short- vs. Long-term
The Alarmists (high risk aversion and high risk perception)	Most likely to respond aggressively; involved politically on the food issue; overinfluence their peers to not take risks	Irrational, overreacting to food issue and risk level; extreme behavior not always justified	Most likely long-term as food habits change drastically to avoid risks
The Conservatives (high risk aversion and low risk perception)	Passive reaction, the "silent majority"; aware of potential risk but no overreaction	Most likely to behave irrationally and not to take any risks because risk-adverse	Short- or long-term, depending on the level of risk aversion
The Concerned (low risk aversion and high risk perception)	Rather passive; will avoid personal risk but won't campaign for it	Most likely to behave irrationally and not to take any risks	Short- or long-term, depending on the level of risk perception
The Accountables (low risk aversion and low risk perception)	Passive behavior; maintain his/her food habits	Rational; ignore information when risk perception is low	Most likely short-term because both perception and aversion of risk are low

Source: Adapted from Wansink 2004a.

rational. Irrational responses can be either more extreme than merited (an overreaction) or less extreme than merited (an underreaction).

Short-Term versus Long-Term Responses   The length of a consumer's response to a problem can be either short term or long term. The response can persist for a short time if the risk has been sufficiently eliminated through structural factors (food inspections or new standards). However, the response can last longer than necessary.

Consider trichinosis. The last case of trichinosis in the United States was reported shortly before World War II, yet the fear still persists in many households today. Although this fear has not influenced current pork sales, pork preparation has been modified in what is perhaps an overly conservative manner, including overcooking. This example illustrates how residue from a food scare can last long after the risk has diminished.

Managing Reactions to Food Crises through Precrisis Preparation

Managing the stigma associated with any food safety issue involves the following precrisis preparations: promote a hierarchical understanding of food production, integrate distinct communication channels, accommodate consumer needs and concerns with packaging and labeling, position products as comparable alternatives, and correctly address public concerns.

Promote a Hierarchical Understanding of Food Production

There are wide differences in the knowledge consumers have about food technology. When combined with the fact that consumers also have different information processing styles, this suggests that the most effective strategies to disseminate food technology information take a stepwise approach. That is, consumers first need to accept the processes of food technology, and only after that will they adopt specific products. Therefore, having information about and confidence in food technology is a necessary condition for acceptance of products made using these technologies.

To accomplish this, a hierarchical model of communication strategy is proposed. As illustrated in Figure 10.2, it is first necessary to disseminate general information such as what food technology is and what would be affected by it. Consumers must have some basic knowledge about food technology in order to process more specific and detailed information.

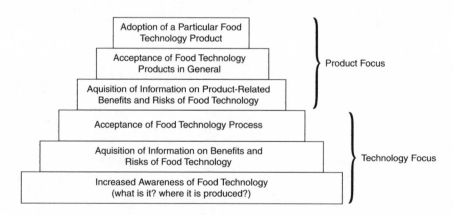

Figure 10.2. Promoting a hierarchical understanding of a new food technology. (Adapted from Wansink and Kim 2001.)

Next, information about food technology used by the specific industries can be communicated and better understood. Once consumers understand and accept the technology or process, information about the benefits and risks involved with products can be more effectively conveyed. This way, consumers will be able to develop a knowledge base on which they can make educated decisions regarding specific food products. Figure 10.2 illustrates how the hierarchy of communication objectives can be structured in relation to the level of consumers' food technology knowledge.

Integrate Distinct Communication Channels

Consumers acquire food safety information from various sources, such as government publications, consumer organizations, research institutes, and the media. Because consumers perceive that there are conflicts between these sources, the resulting confusion can lead to rejection or deferred of acceptance of food technology products. A coordinated communication effort by the multiple information sources is essential in increasing consumer acceptance. Government agencies, universities, other research institutions, the industry, and the media all have a distinct but primary role to play in crisis management.

Consider biotechnology. Although the media have long been a prime information source for consumers, they do not provide much biotechnology information. The effect of the mass media in disseminating biotechnology information has been inhibiting (i.e., distributing news about biohazards) rather than facilitating. A variety of strategies to use mass media as the key information source should be considered. This would include advertising campaigns promoting biotechnology and public relations in the form of articles or programs that disseminate biotechnology information.

Accommodate Consumer Concerns with Packaging and Labeling

There are at least three functions of labeling products: to protect consumer choice, to provide information on product ingredients for health reasons (e.g., allergies), and to encourage companies to provide safer products by requiring disclosure. Although the main function of labels is to provide information, the last function suggests that labeling may function as a cue for product safety. Some consumers may use such labeling to avoid products processed with specific technologies. In contrast, consumers may perceive the explicit labeling as a sign of the manufacturers' confidence in product safety because they are willing to display such information even though disclosure is not required by law.

Care must be taken in how such products are labeled, however. For instance, results of the 1991 Euro-barometer survey reported an interesting finding related to labeling of biotechnology products. The results indicated that the way biotechnology products are labeled influenced both perceptions of and attitudes toward such products. The survey was conducted using a split ballot in which half of the respondents were questioned using the word *biotechnology* and the other half were questioned using the term *genetic engineering*. Twice as many respondents in the "genetic engineering" condition thought that the technology would make their lives worse than did respondents in the "biotechnology" condition. Clearly, consumers have predisposed attitudes toward particular terms such as *genetic engineering*. Regardless of the reasons behind these attitudes, it is important to accommodate the uneasiness the terminology evokes. To do so, manufacturers should seek to avoid the use of potentially negative terms.

Consumers generally view product labeling as an important source of information when developing attitudes toward food technology products. Therefore, labeling and product packaging should reflect the positive aspects of the industry and methods involved in production. Consumer advocacy organizations and research institutions could be used as endorsers for the products or technology because they are viewed as most trustworthy.

In the meantime, it is important to give consumers a sense of control over their choices. Even when consumers are ill-equipped with knowledge, they still want control in choosing what they eat. The use of labeling to provide food technology information should be considered depending on the segment of consumer who is being targeted. Labeling food technology products can serve as both an information source and a safety signal. Food technology communication strategies should give consumers criteria for evaluating food technology products. Consumers will become more comfortable and confident in accepting the technology as their confusion about what and how to choose diminishes.

Position Products as Comparable Alternatives

When contemplating product positioning at the store level, marketers should seek to align products with their nontechnological counterparts. This discourages consumers from seeing the products as "fake" or "synthetic." This is not as important when one is targeting food technology–savvy markets, wherein differentiation techniques can even work as an advantage.

Additionally, efforts should be made to tie in the products with brands and images that are highly regarded and can further reinforce the natural aspects of the food. Through the use of brand equity leveraging, innovative promotion, and product pairing, these products can achieve an air of familiarity, quality, and conventionality.

Correctly Address Public Concerns

Controversy over safety and ethical issues involved in the use of certain misunderstood technologies is a persistent problem. Food technology is advancing into the future, and some of the current safety issues may become nonissues. However, current public concerns are grounded in past abuses, especially regarding biotechnology. Concerns may result partially from the fact that living organisms are adaptive, and changes in their genetic makeup are not completely predictable or controllable.

Therefore, in the long run, the food technology industry, researchers, and government agencies should try to address potential hazards. First, objective measures of potential risks of hazards involved in food technology and related products must be developed. Without such measures, it will be impossible to convince consumers of technology safety. Second, government and industry must put some legal and self-regulatory protection devices in place. Third, and most importantly, a code of ethics that guards against the potential misuse of food and biotechnology must be established and adopted by those who participate in that field. Smart marketers can coordinate with key industry groups to build a wider base of understanding, influence, and safety. Consider the following cooperative efforts.

Self-Regulation by the Food and Biotechnology Industry   Generally, consumers perceive food technology information provided by the industry to be the least credible, and they are most distrustful of an industry-regulated safety system. Therefore, it is critical for the industry to earn consumers' trust. A well-publicized self-regulatory effort by the industry may help gain consumers' confidence. The industry should strive to develop objective measures for the risks and benefits of products and establish self-regulated safety measures for the manufacturing processes.

The Role of Government as the Safeguard   Despite some doubt about the efficiency of government, many focus groups and surveys indicate that consumers believe the government should play an important role in providing regulation and safety protection with respect to food technology. These provisions by the government will alleviate some consumer concerns about food-related issues, particularly biotechnology issues. The government should set the direction and pace of development in order to prevent questionable or premature application of certain food technologies.

University and Research Institutions   Universities and other research institutions account for the majority of genetic engineering and food technology research and development. Therefore, they are well positioned to play a safety assurance role and provide up-to-date information on technological advances and applications. Although industry sponsorship raises some concerns, the public views academic institutions as the most credible and trustworthy source of biotechnological information. This being said, a more active effort to establish and maintain the integrity and impartiality of research by these institutions is important.

Managing Reactions to Food Crises through Postcrisis Responses

The way marketers respond to food crises should take into account whether a country's food consumption is influenced more by risk perceptions or by risk aversion. The relative influence of risk perception and risk aversion on consumption depends on the accuracy of one's assessment of that risk.

Communication Efforts: How Institutions should Respond to Food Crises

If the probability of contracting a disease is not accurately known, research indicates that different policies are appropriate for different types of countries. Consider the BSE crisis. In countries such as the United States, tough measures are needed to prevent a BSE crisis because risk aversion discourages consumption, and little can be done to change it. This means testing and getting rid of suspected food products. In countries such as Germany, both risk perceptions and risk aversion drive consumer behavior. This suggests the need not only for tough measures but also for extensive and responsible dissemination of accurate information by the government, industry, and the media. In contrast to that of the United States and Germany, Dutch consumer behavior is driven mainly by risk perceptions

(Pennings, Wansink, and Muelenberg 2002). In this case, honest and consistent communication by both the government and the food industry is more effective than a mass recall and destruction of food products.

If the probability of contracting a disease is accurately known (or becomes more accurate), risk perception can become a more important driver of food consumption than risk aversion. In low-risk situations, messages from the government, the food industry, and the media will help consumers respond to the food crisis appropriately. In contrast, in high-risk situations tough measures (recall or elimination) are also necessary. In the case of strongly risk-averse consumers, however, any level of risk is treated as high. As a result, tough measures and information are important in even low- and moderate-risk situations. On the production side, an ounce of prevention is worth a pound of cure, but on the policy side, an ounce of information is worth even more.

Risk Management Measures

Risk management measures can be separated into genuine risk management measures and auxiliary risk management measures, or damage control. Only the former should be seriously considered, but the latter is reviewed briefly here.

Genuine risk management measures can focus on systematic hazard removal, based on various food safety systems. In some cases this can involve isolating the cause of the problem. In other cases it can involve eliminating all suspected contaminants. It is important to report these efforts proactively and keep consumers informed about decisions, processes, and progress.

Auxiliary risk management efforts typically involve doing nothing about the problem itself but simply trying to displace negative attention. These efforts often take the form of denial, scapegoating, redefining a hazard, or claiming stakeholder consensus. Otherwise honest people might find themselves reactively relying on such measures in the heat of the moment; forewarned is forearmed.

Dealing with Potential Complications

Even when an emergency response plan is in place, complications can arise. One area in which such complications are common is systematic hazard removal. When existing evidence is poor, Hazard Analysis and Critical Control Point (HACCP) requires extensive risk assessment, which may not be easy to implement. Nevertheless, the resources allocated to risk assessment have important signal value to the public. Depending on the level of resources dedicated to a cause, the public may feel concerned that the risk is higher than initially thought, or they may feel frustrated that nothing is being done. A perceived balance must be maintained.

In some cases, a hazard may turn out to be more severe or more widespread than previously stated. When this occurs, information sources whose previous statements are proven wrong may lose their credibility.

There are also potential drawbacks to proactive consumer information. Information that is intended to educate the public may have unintended signal value, suggesting the existence of previous undisclosed or underestimated hazards. Indeed, information that is intended to restore trust may actually raise consumers' suspicions, pointing to a hidden agenda of the information source. In such a situation, consumers are more likely to stick with the previous risk judgment and trust the information sources only to the degree to which the provided information matches their personal risk judgments.

Lessons for Marketing Nutrition

The rapid growth of food technology and its applications is outpacing consumer understanding. Incomplete understanding of food technology is leading to divided opinions. The theoretical framework presented in this chapter for understanding what factors affect consumers' acceptance of food technology has clear implications for labeling, promoting, publicizing, advertising, and pricing technological food products. A two-phase strategy for managing public opinion—focusing on precrisis interventions and postcrisis responses—is the key planning tool that provides structure for the more tactical efforts.

Four consumer profiles are described in this chapter. People in the accountable segment ignore risk information and keep their habits, even though some risk may be involved. Those in the concerned segment are not risk averse to begin with, so their behavior is determined primarily by their perception of risk. As their perception of the riskiness of an action increases, they approach a point at which they will not participate in the action at all. Those in the conservative segment are cautious, risk-averse consumers who do not take any unnecessary risks. Those in the alarmist segment tend to overreact. Specific efforts targeted at each of these segments are more efficient than broader efforts.

Managing the potential problems associated with any food safety issue involves the following five precrisis preparations: promoting a hierarchical understanding of food production, integrating distinct communication channels, accommodating consumer concerns with packaging and labeling, positioning products as comparable alternatives, and correctly addressing public concerns. Appropriate postcrisis responses include open communication, risk management measures, and dealing with potential complications.

Related Reading

Pennings, J. M. E., B. Wansink, and M. M. E. Meulenberg. "A Note on Modeling Consumer Reactions to a Crisis: The Case of the Mad Cow Disease," *International Journal of Research in Marketing* 19:2 (March 2002): 91–100.

Wansink, B. "Consumer Reactions to Food Safety Crises," *Advances in Food and Nutrition Research* 48 (2004): 103–50.

Wansink, B., and J. Kim. "The Marketing Battle Over Genetically Modified Foods: False Assumptions about Consumer Behavior," *American Behavioral Scientist* 44:8 (April 2001): 1405–17.

PART FOUR

Labeling That Actually Works

ELEVEN

Leveraging Food and Drug Administration Health Claims

"Reduce the risk of heart disease." "Prevent osteoporosis." Health claims such as these might influence our knowledge, but do they motivate us to change our behavior? When do health claims motivate us to eat better? Although effective food labeling and nutritional health claims can have an important impact on consumers, such efforts are not always successful. This chapter examines how the varying degrees of success of U.S. Food and Drug Administration (FDA) health claims provide insights that can help food regulatory agencies in all nations be more effective in their nutrition education and product labeling efforts.

Past research on health claims typically has focused on consumers' perceptions of a health claim's believability, simplicity, or clarity. Taking this a step further, this chapter discusses how we can encourage the consumption of these healthful foods by leveraging health claims effectively. First, I review how consumers learn about health claims and how their awareness of the diet-health relationship influences the acceptance of these claims. Second, I analyze FDA health claims in the context of consumer learning. Finally, I illustrate the implications of nutritional education and product labeling in the context of soy health claims.

How Consumers Learn about Health Claims

Consumers receive information about health claims from a variety of sources. Product nutritional labels are a primary source of this information, followed by point-of-purchase displays, special educational campaigns, friends, family, and health professionals. Sometimes, however, consumers see such information as misleading or unclear, and it has increasingly become important for other sources (such as academia, public health communities, and medical practitioners) to lend credibility to health claims. In addition, government agencies have been important in helping broaden the reach of nutritional and health messages, particularly when teamed in strategic partnerships. For example, the National Cancer Institute's "Five-a-Day" campaign to increase fruit and vegetable consumption was conducted in partnership with the Produce for Better Health Foundation. This is growing evidence of the possibilities of public-private partnerships and of national-local partnerships.

In the case of FDA-approved health claims, many consumers feel that the claims are too vague, wordy, academic, and long. The Nutrition Labeling and Education Act changed the way nutritional information is presented on food labels, making the information more useful and informative. Still, it is often suggested that consumers neither comprehend nor use nutritional information in their food purchase decisions because they are skeptical of health claims or perceive them as incomplete or misleading.

However, there are instances in which consumers can accurately evaluate health claims and information from the nutritional fact panel. By building on these past successes, marketers can develop, format, and disseminate health claims in a way that facilitates a consumer's interpretation, belief, and use of information on product labels.

Knowledge about nutrition influences eating habits only when a person is motivated to act on it. The most common form of motivation is one that ties a consumer's general knowledge about how nutrition influences health with his or her knowledge of the nutrient content of a particular type of food. Indeed, awareness of a relationship between diet and health is commonly cited as the primary factor that leads to positive changes in a person's diet.

At a basic level, there are two types of knowledge consumers can have about nutrition. First, they can have knowledge about a particular product's nutritional properties, such as vitamin A content or cholesterol levels. Second, they can have knowledge about how these nutritional properties affect health. The understanding that a diet low in cholesterol helps prevent heart disease or that a diet high in vitamin A helps vision are both examples of this second type of knowledge (Wansink, Westgren, and Cheney 2005).

When both of these types of knowledge are jointly present, a higher level of understanding occurs. Because the consumer knows that a certain type of food contains certain nutritional properties and that those properties produce certain health benefits, the consumer is able to conclude that this food will lead to certain health benefits. This awareness of the connections between diet and health can help provide the motivation to consume recommended foods.

Through their placement and wording, FDA health claims are intended to inform consumers of the important connection between diet and health. Yet in many cases consumers simply do not believe this connection. It is important for consumers to know the nutrient content of food and how certain nutritional aspects affect health before they can draw the connection between diet and health. If consumers are unaware that a food contains certain nutritional qualities and that certain nutritional qualities influence health, convincing them of an FDA health claim will be difficult. This is because the consumer lacks the background and confidence to change his or her dietary habits in a manner consistent with the information in the health claim.

Five Lessons from Successful FDA Claims

Examining successful FDA health claims enables us to determine what made these claims effective in persuading consumers. Knowing why some health claims are more effective than others will reveal guidelines for developing marketing communications.

Target a Specific Group

Consider the FDA health claim about calcium and osteoporosis: "Regular exercise and a healthy diet with enough calcium helps teens and young adults, white and Asian women maintain good bone health and may reduce their high risk of osteoporosis later in life." In general, this claim is thought to have increased dairy sales. One reason is that most products carrying the FDA label have either been fortified with calcium (and labeled accordingly) or they are products traditionally associated with calcium (such as milk). The connection between the product and the calcium is strong. A second reason is that products carrying the FDA label about calcium draw on a long history of the benefits of calcium, based on prior education and marketing programs. The combined awareness of calcium in the product and awareness of calcium's positive nutritional benefit caused the FDA label to be well received.

This illustrates the success of a health claim that applies to a specifically defined segment of the population. Unlike more broadly targeted claims, the calcium claim specifically targets the very young and the very old. As the success of the calcium claim demonstrates, when a particular group of beneficiaries is specified, the claim becomes more believable and hence more successful.

Seek Media Attention

The FDA health claims relating to fat and cancer and to saturated fat, cholesterol, and heart disease received a great deal of attention, particularly in the late 1990s. The FDA claim for fat and cancer is, "Development of cancer depends on many factors. A diet low in fat may reduce the risk of some cancers," and the claim for saturated fat, cholesterol, and heart disease is, "While many factors affect heart disease, diets low in saturated fat and cholesterol may reduce the risk of this disease." Products such as fruits, vegetables, low-fat milk products, cereals, pastas, flours, whole grain, and sherbets have all benefited from these two claims.

This success can be attributed partially to the two necessary criteria described in the basic framework. First, as a result of the nutritional label requirement, consumers were able to quickly identify the amount and type of fat in all products. Second, federally sponsored commodity programs and the "Five-a-Day for Better Health" program (along with a general societal concern of obesity) have all contributed to the connection consumers make between fat intake and health. The combination of both types of information helped make these two FDA fat health claims successful.

This example illustrates the success that a health claim can achieve when it receives media attention. Focused media attention increased consumer awareness of the fat content of their favorite foods, and it increased awareness of the negative consequences of fat consumption. Media attention augmented consumers' diet-health relationship awareness and helped decrease the consumption of high-fat products.

Find Corporate Partners to Copromote the Claim

Two FDA claims deal with the link between fiber and heart disease and between fiber and some types of cancer. These claims focus primarily on whole-grain breads and cereals, fruits, and vegetables. The claim for the fiber and cancer link is, "Low-fat diets rich in fiber-containing grain products, fruits, and vegetables may reduce the risk of some types of cancer, a disease associated with many factors." The claim for the fiber and heart disease link is, "Diets low in saturated fat and cholesterol and rich in fruits, vegetables, and grain products that contain some types of dietary fiber, particularly soluble fiber, may reduce the risk of heart disease, a disease associated with many factors."

The success of these health claims mirrors the success of those already mentioned. First, as a result of intense education about fiber through the Food Pyramid program, consumer awareness of fiber in the foods they buy increased. Second, the link between high-fiber diets and good health has been facilitated by proactive campaigns from companies such as Quaker Oats and Kellogg's, which informed consumers about the benefits of fiber and the presence of fiber in their cereals. In one instance, the National Cancer Institute lent its credibility to an educational campaign conducted by the Kellogg's company. Both consumer awareness of fiber in the foods and the awareness of the health benefits to fiber made these two health claims successful.

When a health claim's introduction is accompanied by a proactive marketing campaign that targets the link between a nutrient and good health, substantial success can be achieved. In much the same way that media attention leverages a health claim, a marketing campaign directly informs consumers of a nutrient's affect on health.

Focus on Quantifiable or Observable Results

The link between sodium and high blood pressure also has received FDA approval, with the health claim, "Diets low in sodium may reduce the risk of high blood pressure, a disease associated with many factors." Products that have low sodium content, such as unsalted tuna, salmon, fruits, vegetables, low-fat milk and yogurt, cottage cheese, cereal, flour, and pasta, are positively affected by this health claim. Success in this area can be attributed to consumer awareness of sodium in foods and high awareness of the role of sodium in heart disease.

The success of this health claim illustrates the value of a health benefit that is quantifiable and easily observable. A health claim that can provide a quantifiable benefit such as lower blood pressure is more likely to increase consumption than a more intangible claim.

Make a Claim Personal

Fruits and vegetables have been linked with lowering the risk of some types of cancer, and the related claim generally states, "Low-fat diets rich in fruits and vegetables (foods that are low in fat and may contain dietary fiber, vitamin A, or vitamin C) may reduce the risk of some types of cancer, a disease associated with many factors. Broccoli is high in vitamin A and C, and it is a good source of dietary fiber." A strong connection between the bioactive ingredients in fruits and vegetables and the effect of those bioactive ingredients on cancer contributes to the success of this claim. Many consumers have a close family member or friend who has heart disease. A health claim that can prevent this disease becomes more potent and more successful as a result of the personal connection.

Table 11.1 reviews the principles behind these successful health claims and provides lessons that can be useful for future claims.

Table 11.1. Principles to Successfully Leverage Health Claims

Principle	Benefits	Examples
Claim targets a specific segment of the population	Makes claim more believable; draws attention of focused consumer groups	Calcium's focused claim on the very young and the very old; folic acid claim targeting pregnant mothers
Claim has received significant media attention	Informs consumers of a relationship between a certain nutrient and health; makes claim more believable and authentic	Fat and saturated fat health claims linking low fat diets with decreased risk of cancer
Claim's introduction is done with an aggressive pro-active marketing campaign	Informs consumers of a nutrient's health benefit; informs consumers of a specific product containing that nutrient	Quaker Oats and Kellogg's marketing campaign highlighting the link between fiber and a low risk of heart disease
Claim can highlight the quantitative health benefits	Allows consumers to see health claim actually improving health; increases believability when initial consumers relate that the health claim is correct	Sodium health claims linking a diet low in sodium to a low blood pressure number
Claim helps prevent a health problem many consumers have a personal relationship with	Makes health claim more believable and realistic; increases awareness of the risks associated with diets lacking beneficial nutrient	Heart disease health claims linking diets rich in fruits and vegetables to a decreased risk of cancer

Source: Adapted from Wansink 2005.

Why Are Some FDA Claims Less Successful?

The final health claim we will examine links folic acid with neural tube birth defects and states, "Healthful diets with adequate folate may reduce a woman's risk of having a child with a brain or spinal cord birth defect." Many foods naturally contain folic acid, including enriched cereal grain products, some legumes, peas, fresh leafy green vegetables, oranges, grapefruit, and many berries.

This claim did not generate the type of success seen with the aforementioned health claims. Unlike calcium and fiber, folate has not acquired the same level of awareness. In fact, consumers typically do not know what foods contain folate. Marketers selling products with this claim have used folate fortification to increase the visibility of folate in their foods. In addition, unlike heart disease and cancer, spinal cord birth defects affect only a small number of people. This limits the public's awareness of the effects of folate and has hampered the success of this FDA claim among the target population.

The lower level of success of this claim in increasing the consumption of foods with folic acid allows us to use it to illustrate, by negative example, the factors that contribute to a successful health claim. First, unlike obesity, which has received media attention, neural tube birth defects are a lesser-known problem. The result is that consumers faced with this health claim had less incentive to act on it. Second, unlike Quaker Oats, which sponsored a proactive marketing campaign highlighting the benefits of fiber, folic acid producers did not sponsor a similar campaign with their products. Therefore, whereas consumers were well aware of the benefits of fiber, they were less aware of the benefits of folic acid. Third, unlike blood pressure, neural tube birth defects are less visible and quantifiable. That is, whereas consumers could clearly see the benefits of a low-sodium diet (and tell their friends about it), they could not easily see the benefits of folic acid. Fourth, whereas many people have a family connection with heart disease, most are unfamiliar with neural tube birth defects. Therefore, whereas fruit and vegetable growers can market their products as preventing a disease that many consumers know from personal experience, the marketers of products containing folic acid can not. Finally, the success the folic acid health claim has achieved can be attributed to the leveraging ability it derived from having a specific focus group of consumers affected by the health claim: pregnant women (Table 11.1).

Labeling Is Not Enough

Food labels are important in helping consumers recognize that a product contains a particular nutrient. These labeling efforts appear to be most effective when combined with consumer education, advertising, and public relations efforts. Aside from nutritional content, food labels also help signal product quality, consumer knowledge, purchasing patterns, and usage patterns. Despite its tremendous influence, labeling alone is not always persuasive. Many consumers rarely look at nutritional information, and some who do so do not believe the labels. Special attention should be paid to consumers' perceptions, beliefs, attitudes, values, and social influences in creating a nutritional label that will be understood and believed. Recent work has shown that combining short health claims on the front of a package with full health claims on the back of the package can lead consumers to more fully process and believe the claim (Wansink, Sonka, and Hasler 2005). This finding is relevant for policymakers, consumers, and researchers.

Long-term behavioral change can be achieved only through a cohesive effort. Food developers and package designers should create a system of labeling (coupled with education) to alert consumers of the nutritional contents of a particular product.

Implications for Nutrition Education

Many consumers believe a health claim is accurate if it appears on the food label. Although consumers have a positive attitude toward health messages on food labels, they do not always understand them well. Also, research shows that consumers associate an individual nutrient with certain diseases but are not knowledgeable about specifics of that nutrient (i.e., recommended intakes, sources, functions, or classifications). Nutrition experts play an ongoing role in providing accurate nutrition education to the public.

Consumers have gotten the message regarding existing health claims. However, many nutrition education efforts emphasize instrumental knowledge transfer, with insufficient attention to achieving behavior change. Nutrition education is the best way to achieve the desired behavior change. Such education should have a strong consumer orientation; segment and target specific consumer groups; use multiple, mutually reinforcing, interactive channels of communication; and continually refine the consumer message.

Historically, new foods and technologies that have been developed to improve nutritional content have not been accompanied by national nutrition efforts. The industry must build new partnerships in order to attain behavior change. These partnerships are necessary because the food industry alone cannot change consumer behavior. Conducting clinical trials to conclusively demonstrate health benefits has traditionally been the domain of the pharmaceutical and medical industries, but they are only necessary adjuncts to food products sold for their health benefits. It is time for food organizations (such as trade associations) to also participate in such trials.

Communication with the medical community traditionally has been limited to specialty food companies marketing medical foods, but an educational campaign for health care professionals can be important in helping build credibility and more widespread consumer acceptance of various foods. Medical professionals are positioned to identify the consumers who are most likely to be interested in adopting specific recommended foods. The industry must provide these professionals with detailed information on the foods available and how they should best be consumed.

Related trade associations must also develop partnerships with pertinent government and public health organizations. Such organizations will help provide the funding and communication venues needed to deliver messages. Health communities also have the best ideas on how to change behavior because they can personalize messages to meet their audience's needs. For instance, because of the link between cancer and heart disease, soy associations have strong natural allies that are already recognizable to consumers as credible organizations.

An Illustration of How FDA Claims Can Be Leveraged

To see how these claims can be leveraged, consider the health claim detailing the link between soy protein and heart disease and cancer. Leveraging the past mistakes of FDA health claims and building on past successes can increase consumption of products carrying the soy health claim. Soy protein is still in the crucial emerging stage of consumer acceptance, so soy marketers and manufacturers have the luxury of a reasonably clean slate. However, the groundwork laid at this stage of health promotion can promote or limit the long-term success of a health claim program. As indicated in Table 11.2, the strategy to bring soy protein to the forefront must include nutrition education and promotion, in accordance with the insights described in this chapter.

Table 11.2. Implications for Leveraging FDA-Approved Health Benefits: A Soy Illustration

Context of Use	Guidelines	Reasons and Examples
Education	• Design clinical studies for health professionals • Implement social marketing campaigns • Educate consumers on ease of product use • Develop education programs for nutrition educators on how to change the motivations of potential consumers	• Exhibit advantages to professionals; supply them with products and ways to educate their patients • Good publicity for firm who develops social campaigns • Provide recipes and where to find products
Promotion	• Use Five-a-Day program • Copromote with heart and cancer associations • Use point-of-sale reminders of health benefits	• "Soy is a vital part of your Five-a-Day program." • "The AHA recommends 20 grams of soy a day. This product contains 100% of daily recommendations."
Packaging	• Do not use words that cannot easily be quantified • Keep phrases simple on front and link to nutrition panel for credibility	• Use words such as *less, more, reduced, percentages,* and *quantities* • Do not need to include "As a part of a balanced diet" anymore. Try wording such as "Packed with Soy Protein." • Have heart check and cancer association symbols easily visible. Include a soy symbol alongside to build awareness and credibility.
Placement	• Health food stores • Place with comparable products in grocery stores • Doctor's and health-care offices • Gyms	• Avoid placement in special section of supermarket (focus on general public) • Place in outlets where the fact that the product is there implies its health benefits
Product	• Include readily identifiable symbols of affiliation • Fortify existing products • Fortify products through line extensions	• Add soy to diets of people that wouldn't necessarily purchase soy products • Give existing products a soy line as an option.
Pricing	• Price high for special products that promote their inclusion of soy • Initially price lower than competing products to encourage adoption	• Do not want to give soy a cheap image so when people become more affluent, they won't move away from product • Emphasize price and health benefit combination ("Eat healthy for the same price")

Source: Adapted from Wansink 2005.

Lessons for Marketing Nutrition

To change any behavior, the key is to establish behavior change as a goal, incorporate motivating communications, teach strategies for behavior change, and encourage a health-enhancing environment. With these general principles in mind, let us examine their relationship to health claims.

Health claims can influence consumer behavior when the following conditions exist. First, the consumer must be made aware that the product carrying the health claim possesses the target nutrient. Second, the consumer must be made aware that the particular nutrient provides a health benefit. A combination of these two factors establishes a clear diet-health relationship between a particular product and a particular health benefit. This can motivate the consumption of that particular product.

Although all products that establish a diet-health relationship have the potential to influence consumer behavior, it takes an extra level of motivation to translate that potential into action. Past health claims provide clear examples of principles that can be used to leverage health claims and make them more successful. Future health claims should capitalize and build on the five lessons of the FDA health claims discussed here: target a specific group, seek media attention, find corporate partners to copromote the claim, focus on quantitative or observable results, and make a claim personal.

From a marketing nutrition perspective, placing a health message on a product can add value to the promotion and position of the product, but only if it is well targeted, widely communicated, and copromoted through a wide variety of channels. Last, its effects should be observable and personal. Although the claim itself is a product of science, its overall effectiveness is a product of marketing.

Related Reading

Wansink, B., and M. M. Cheney. "Leveraging FDA Claims," *Journal of Consumer Affairs,* forthcoming.

TWELVE

Health Claims: When Less Equals More

Should we make health claims lengthy and complete or catchy and quick? A longer, more complete health claim is most accurate, but a shorter one can be more easily processed and more persuasive. The concerns over Food and Drug Administration (FDA) claims being accurate but misunderstood are well founded. Although the Nutrition Labeling and Education Act was intended to make food labels more useful and informative, consumers still do not always comprehend nutritional information. Many are skeptical of health claims, and they believe such claims are incomplete, misleading, or trivial. Part of the problem may be the way in which such information is formatted. In some cases too much information overwhelms consumers, and in other cases too little misleads them.

In general, consumers are thought to view front label information as a summary of a product's benefits or hazards. Presumably, if they found interesting or important information incompletely described on the front of a product, they would be motivated to seek clarification on other parts of the package. Unfortunately, some consumers who are casually skimming a front label might take away only a top-line summary. The more difficult this front label information is to comprehend quickly, the more likely it is to be ignored or misinterpreted. Nutrition-conscious consumers may be more likely to examine all sides of a package in detail. Effective nutrition labels should take both less-involved and more-involved shoppers into account. One way to address the different information needs of both groups would be to print health claim information on both the front and back labels of a package.

One combination of information that might be appropriate for a wide range of consumers would involve back panel information that provides complete nutritional details and front panel information that provides a brief summary of these details. In such a case, a casual shopper could skim the front and have a basic understanding of the claim, and a more involved shopper could find detailed information on the back of the package. The presence of a short claim on the front label makes it easier to process attribute-specific product information. To the extent that this information is unambiguous, it should improve the persuasiveness of the health claims.

Because we know that health claims on the front panel of a package can influence purchase behavior, the question becomes how much front panel information is needed to persuasively communicate the health benefits or hazards of a product. After reviewing how nutrition label information might be processed, I compare consumers who are exposed to different health claim combinations on the front and back of labels.

How Do Consumers Read Labels?

Labeling can influence perceptions, preferences, prepurchase expectations, and posttrial evaluations, but too much information can lead consumers to become confused and to make poor decisions. Understanding the ideal amount of purchase-relevant information has been a major concern of both policymakers and marketing researchers. The value of label information hinges on the availability, complexity, and relevance of the information provided to consumers through packaging and advertising. If too much information is provided to consumers in a complicated format, they are less likely to use it effectively.

There has been concern that as labels become more complicated, people pay less attention to them. Indeed, a HealthFocus (2003) study investigated how important labels were in communicating information about fat, calories, sugar, sodium, and other characteristics (Figure 12.1). In all of these categories, the percentage of people who said that a label's claim was an extremely or very important source of information has steadily dropped since 1994. Less than 40 percent viewed labels as important sources of information.

Consumers may ignore excessive amounts of information. However,

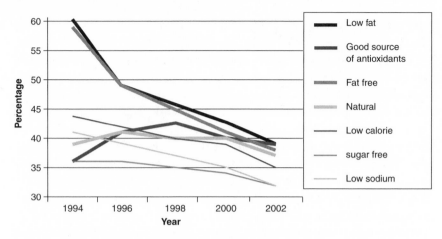

Figure 12.1. Percentage of respondents saying label claims are extremely or very important. (Health Focus 2003.)

if consumers view front panel information as a summary of the package, simplified, shorter claims on the front panel may make health claims more easily understood and more persuasive. A concern with long health claims is that people do not understand them, and a concern of short health claims is that people can be misled by them. Having a short claim on the front can give all consumers a general idea of the health claim, and it prompts interested consumers to evaluate the full claim information on back. Because some people are likely to ignore a longer health claim on the front, it is less likely to be believed than a shorter claim. To the extent that these claims are perceived as favorable, this increased level of attribute-specific processing is likely to make shorter claims more persuasive.

Short front panel claims increase the believability of health claims. However, seeing a shorter claim may lead the consumer to believe he or she already understands the claim and therefore to less carefully scrutinize the back panel. This could lead to an inaccurate understanding of the claims. The same mechanism that generates specific thoughts about a product may also lead one to infer traits or benefits that seem reasonable but are false.

The Battle of the Health Claims

To determine how the length of front panel information influences consumers, we compared three modified packages for soy protein patties. To make the task as realistic as possible, we modified an existing but unfamiliar product package. Three different nutrition label conditions were used (Table 12.1): The front label of the product featured either a shorter soy health claim, a longer soy health claim, or no claim (control condition). A complete soy health claim and the standard nutrition information were provided on the back panel in all three conditions.

At the beginning of the study, we told 165 adults that some new concept products were being developed and that we would like to know their impressions of them. Each person was shown two distractor products before being given the target product. They were then given a questionnaire that asked them to write down the thoughts (cognitive responses) they had when examining the product.

After this, each participant was asked about various health benefits of the product. We used three target claims to test the impact of labeling on claim believability by asking participants to rate three statements ("People would benefit from eating this product," "This product may reduce the risk of heart disease," and "This should be eaten with a low saturated fat diet"). In addition, one claim that researchers currently believe to be false ("This product can help counteract less healthy food") was included to explore whether the same process that makes claims more believable may also lead to inaccuracies.

Table 12.1. Examples of Front and Back Panel Health Claims: Experimental Treatments

	Type of Claim	Claim
Front panel	None	
	Short	"Soy protein may help reduce the risk of heart disease. See back panel for nutrition information."
	Long	"Soy protein, as part of a diet low in saturated fat and cholesterol, may help reduce the risk of heart disease. See back panel for nutrition information"
Back panel	Complete Soy Health Claim (with a standard nutrition facts information panel)	"25 grams of soy protein a day, as a part of a diet low in saturated fat and cholesterol, may help reduce the risk of heart disease. A serving of Harvest Burger provides 16 grams of soy protein"

Source: Wansink (2001).

Short Claims Cause People to Think about the Specific Claims

Consumers who saw short claims on the front of a package generated a greater number of attribute-specific thoughts (e.g., "this is high in protein") and fewer general evaluative thoughts (e.g., "this is good") about the product than those seeing a longer claim. General evaluative thoughts are typically associated with less involved and less effortful thinking than are attribute-specific thoughts. Indeed, the number of attribute-specific thoughts generated by the consumers in the long claim condition was similar to that of the condition in which no claim information was given.

Analyzing the number and type of thoughts one generates when reading a package label helps us better assess whether consumers are making general evaluations or specific attribute-level observations. Although all three front label conditions generated a similar number of thoughts, the nature of these thoughts varied significantly. In general, those seeing a shorter claim on a front label generated fewer general thoughts and more attribute-specific thoughts than those seeing a longer claim. To marketers of nutrition, this is important because it means people who see shorter health claims will find them more persuasive than those who see longer claims or no health claims.

Short Claims Are More Believable

One consequence of favorable attribute-specific processing is that it increases the believability and persuasiveness of the relevant claims. The results (Figure 12.2) indicate that a simplified, shorter health claim led consumers to believe that people would benefit from eating the product. We found the same general pattern when we asked participants whether they agreed with the statement, "This product may reduce the risk of heart disease."

In this context, it is also important to note the extent to which consumers misinterpret health claims and infer unmerited benefits. In some cases, products with health claims may appear to have a "magic pill" quality. That is, they can wrongly be believed to accomplish much more than they can. To examine this possibility, we asked respondents whether they agreed with the statement "This product can help counteract less healthy foods." Although it is incorrect, people in both the short claim and the long claim conditions tended to believe that the product would help counteract their eating of less healthful foods. The length of the health claim had no effect on whether they believed that the product should be eaten in combination with a low–saturated fat diet.

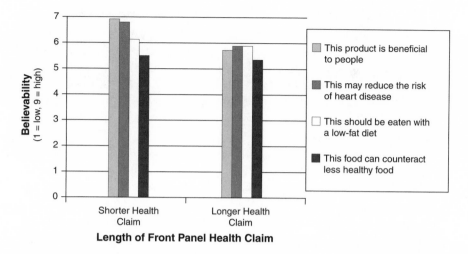

Figure 12.2. Shorter health claims are more believable.

Exit interviews helped explain why short health claims on a front panel in combination with a complete claim on back can influence a consumer's evaluation of a product. In these interviews, consumers noted that the shorter claim helped them better understand the product's health benefits without providing so much information that they lost interest. This proved to be important because many consumers did not spend much time reading the package, and the longer claims often were the items that they claimed to skim.

Use Both Sides of the Package but Use Different Claims

How do the different formats of health claims on the front of a package influence the thoughts consumers generate and the believability of a health label? These results suggest that combining short health claims on the front of a package with full health claims on the back of the package leads consumers to more fully process and believe the claim. In doing so, these results support the proponents of shorter claims and labels.

The basic finding that using two sides of a package (short claim on front, long on back) increases the believability of health claims is relevant for policymakers, consumers, and researchers. Policymakers may find it interesting that shorter health claims on the front panel led to better believability of the product benefits than did the longer claims. Consider the case of the FDA claim about soy protein. Some lawmakers argued that a longer, more complete health claim would be most accurate, whereas others argued that a shorter claim would be more effective. Although the longer, more complete health claim is currently in place, its effectiveness is lower if consumers ignore it or do not understand it. Because short health claims on the front label of a package appear to increase the believability of claims, such claims may also influence purchase or consumption behavior.

Most labeling studies focus only on the claims placed on one side of a label. Using only one side of the label appears to limit a product's ability to communicate its health benefits to both the less involved shopper and the more involved one. Whereas some consumers simply skim the label of a product, others read it more closely. Using both sides of a package provides access to two different audiences. The longer, more comprehensive back label claims provide the details more involved consumers seek. The shorter front label claims provide the ease of processing that less involved consumers seek. Although the abbreviated claim offers a persuasive shortcut for processing product information, it may lead to inaccurate inferences.

In an effort to generalize this research, we included a wide cross-section of age, income, and education levels in the sample. Although all consumers were from the same geographic area, there is no reason to believe that general processing tendencies would vary significantly across geographic regions. However, it is likely that short claims would become even more effective with less educated consumers. It is also likely that the difference in label effectiveness would have been greater in an in-store situation. In an actual shopping situation, time-pressured shoppers might be even more likely to skim the label. This would further necessitate the importance of having a short claim on the front of the package.

More information is not always better for all people, nor is it best for all products. Although it is necessary to provide full information on packages, it may be more effective to provide full information on the back panel, combined with an abbreviated claim on front. If there is only minor risk of a food label being misinterpreted, the increased believability of using front and back labels might be well worth the risk. However, for pharmaceutical products, a misinterpretation of shorter labels may cause grave harm.

Lessons for Marketing Nutrition

An issue of emerging importance to researchers, marketers, and policy-makers is how the length of a claim on the front of a package influences consumer beliefs. In addition to improving our understanding of consumer behavior, these results suggest that the presence of short health claims on the front panel of a product may generate attribute-related positive thoughts that communicate beneficial aspects of the product. Our results also suggest that consumers generate more positive inferences from short claims than from long claims on the front panel. This suggests that short claims on the front panel may provide consumers more understanding of the attributes or benefits of the product. These findings have relevance for policymakers, marketers, and researchers.

First, policymakers may find it interesting that in this study, short claims on the front panel performed better than did long claims. If a short claim on the front panel provides accurate and relevant information, consumers are more likely to understand and believe the health claim. Many consumers limit their information search to the front label, so a positive bias occurs when health claims are present. Thus, policymakers can accomplish their purpose of consumer education, and consumers can benefit from the presence of a shorter health claim on the front panel.

Second, with the presence of a short claim on the front panel, marketers may increase the understandability and believability of product claims. The use of short claims on the front panel may provide consumers at the point of purchase with another type of promotional message that anchors their initial perception of a product. This is significant because it tells marketers how to approach product placement and packaging. We can establish a meaningful reach with consumers through short marketing messages on the product, and point-of-purchase sales with even a short exposure may influence a positive perception of the product.

This study also tells us that we don't need to overload the consumer with information; in fact, too much information may have a negative effect. We learned from chapter 1 that it is not how much consumers know but what they know that makes a difference. Taking this a step further, this chapter reveals how the product messages should be presented to help consumers understand and use the information.

Related Readings

This chapter summarizes a series of research studies on the topic of labeling. Two representative studies on which this chapter is based provides more details about the specific types of thoughts that are generated by different configurations of labels, both in the lab and in in-store tests.

Wansink, Brian. "Do Front and Back Package Labels Influence Beliefs about Health Claims?" *Journal of Consumer Affairs* 37:2 (December 2003a): 171–86.

PART FIVE

Marketing Nutrition

THIRTEEN

Introducing Unfamiliar Foods to Unfamiliar Lands

If we look at food consumption patterns, we see that they are greatly affected by cultural differences. How do we encourage people to alter their consumption patterns and consume an unfamiliar food that could meet a key nutritional need? When developing a marketing strategy around a functional food, it is important to consider the cultural context and perceptions that may cause consumers to resist trying unfamiliar foods. This chapter offers a better understanding of consumer behavior, which will allow us to make marketing decisions that will lead to new food adoption and effective marketing of nutrition.

During the rationing years of World War II, American citizens were encouraged to incorporate protein-rich organ meats into their protein-deficient diets. Initial attempts to change their consumption behavior were rejected because the preparation and the taste of organ meats were unfamiliar. Similarly, although today's protein deficiencies throughout the world could be inexpensively reduced with soy protein, use of soy is widely rejected because the preparation and the taste of soy are unfamiliar.

The acceptance of an unfamiliar food depends on it being made to appear consistent with cultural perceptions and consumption patterns. To better understand the process by which food is accepted and integrated into a particular culture, we present a framework based on two critical factors that influence acceptance of an unfamiliar food. The first is the strength of cultural attitudes and traditions in daily life. Hofstede (1980) refers to cultures whose traditions and practices strongly affect daily life as higher-context cultures, whereas those whose cultural traditions and practices only weakly affect daily life are referred to as lower-context cultures. The second factor we examine is the general perception of food consumption within a culture. Some cultures view food exclusively as providing nutrition (utilitarian cultures), whereas others have a greater appreciation for the complexity of preparation and for the process of savoring food (hedonic cultures).

Thinking of food acceptance in terms of cultural attitude and general food perception is important in our efforts to market nutrition because it improves our understanding of how to integrate new foods into different cultures. Using this framework, we can develop strategies for effectively encouraging the acceptance of any unfamiliar food. More generally, however, this framework improves our understanding of how culture influences food consumption.

After outlining the components of this framework, I use it to examine how soy could most effectively be introduced to Russia and Colombia. Then I provide general guidelines to show how this framework can be used to offer insights related to distribution, message positioning, and marketing strategy for other foods and products in a variety of situations.

How Cultural Context Influences Food Preference

A person's acceptance of a new food type depends greatly on his or her culture. If a person believes that an unfamiliar food can be easily integrated into that person's diet and culture, the food is likely to be accepted. The likelihood of an unfamiliar food being integrated into a culture depends on whether the context of a culture is high or low. Higher-context cultures, such as those often found in Latin America and Asia, focus heavily on personal relationships and social interaction. In contrast, lower-context cultures, such as those of many Western nations, focus on individualism and achievement. Table 13.1 describes how a culture's context can affect how people make decisions.

The same characteristics that influence personal choices also influence food choices. Just as higher-context cultures favor cultural traditions and practices, these cultures also favor foods and dining rituals that have cultural significance. For example, in the higher–cultural context nation of Colombia, the traditional Colombian tortilla (the *arepa*) is favored over imported tortillas. As a result of their individualism, lower-context cul-

Table 13.1. Characteristics of Higher- and Lower-Context Cultures

Area of Impact	Higher-Context Cultures	Lower-Context Cultures
Personal choice	• Strong preference toward cultural traditions and practices • Desire for many close personal relationships with family, friends, co-workers, and clients • Tendency to use multiple forms of communication at once (e.g., tone of voice, timing, facial expressions, and choice of words) • Focus on meaning that is implicit in relationships and situations • Placement of emphasis on the group (e.g., collectivism)	• Strong preference toward individual decisions and preferences • Lack of strong cultural pressure to follow tradition • Tendency to use explicit and straightforward communication (e.g., complete, accurate, and appropriate word choice) • Placement of emphasis on the individual • Willingness to change cultural patterns
Food choice	• Value placed on traditional food dishes • Considers food presentation and texture to be as important as taste • Preference for complex and involved food dishes • Unwilling to try foreign and not culturally accepted foods • Tendency to favor taste over nutrition	• Value placed on functional, practical, nutritional foods • Preference for simple, quick food dishes • High willingness to accept new foods and adapt personal eating habits accordingly

Source: Wansink, Sonka, and Cheney (2002).

tures do not have this level of cultural attachment and tend to prefer foods that are inexpensive, simple, and convenient to prepare.

Table 13.1 lists some of the general themes of lower-context and higher-context cultures. For the most part, higher-context cultures include countries in Latin America and Asia, such as the culturally rich and personally interactive Colombian culture. As a result of its higher context, Colombia has a strong emphasis on cultural foods and complex dishes. Lower-context cultures include Anglo-Saxon cultures and those in Eastern Europe. For instance, Russia is generally a much more individualist culture (despite its historically collectivist government) with a strong emphasis on straightforward communication. As a result, Russia deals with more practical food matters and places greater emphasis on individual decision making. Colombia and Russia are used in this chapter to highlight the extreme ends of the cultural context continuum.

Different Views of Eating

All cultures do not consume food for the same reasons. Some cultures view food consumption as a necessary task to stay healthy; others view it as a highly refined and culturally expressive activity. The former group of cultures can be generally categorized as utilitarian cultures, and the latter group of cultures (with cultural expression as a central aspect of food consumption) can be viewed as more hedonic cultures. Although these categorizations are only generalities, Table 13.2 outlines key differences to underscore how this distinction has been useful in explaining a wide range of behaviors in other contexts.

Consider Vietnam. As a result of food shortages and civil strife, food consumption has become focused on providing nutritional and health benefits, making Vietnam a utilitarian culture. The people of Vietnam view food primarily as a functional instrument that provides value by being a means to an end. A hedonic culture, such as the Japanese culture, views food as experiential and affective; food is appreciated for its own sake, with less regard for its practical characteristics.

This division between utilitarian and hedonic cultures provides an important distinction in cultural perceptions of food. Hedonic cultures treat food consumption as a deeply cultural experience involving meaningful, complex preparation and enjoyment. In a hedonic culture such as that of Colombia, cultural traditions play an integral part in determin-

Table 13.2. Characterizing Utilitarian and Hedonic Perceptions of Food Consumption

Utilitarian Perception	Hedonic Perception
Emphasis on functional aspects of food	Emphasis on the taste of food
Preference toward simple cultural foods and dishes	Preference for cultural eating practices
Desire for practicality in food consumption	Desire for complex cultural food dishes or for elaborate and extravagant foods
Focus on the end benefits of eating food such as energy, calories, or nutrition	Focus on the cultural practice of eating food as well as the end benefits

Source: Wansink, Sonka, and Cheney (2002).

ing a person's diet. Utilitarian cultures, on the other hand, perceive food consumption as more simply related to nutritional and health benefits. In a utilitarian culture such as that of Russia, food is valued primarily as a means to an end.

Why Do Different Countries Like Different Foods?

The resulting matrix of cultural context and perceptions of food consumption provides us with a framework that can help us understand why different countries like different foods and can help us predict the size of the market for a new food product. In addition, the framework is a useful tool for determining how to encourage the adoption of new foods. I use soy as an example because it is a healthful, inexpensive, versatile, and unfamiliar food in many parts of the world, including Russia and Colombia.

Example 1: Introducing Soy-Fortified Foods to Russia

Introducing an unfamiliar food into Russia entails taking into account both the lower cultural context and utilitarian cultural perception of food in Russia. Russian culture emphasizes the practical and functional elements of food. Therefore, it is less important to encourage Russians to culturally desire soy than it is to simply introduce it as a cost-effective, nutritious, functional means of fortifying existing foods.

Although many foods can be fortified with soy, some soy-fortified products will be accepted more easily than others. Factors such as how soy will affect the nutritional value and price of soy-fortified foods are critically important in making the decision about which products should be fortified first. Meat may be the best candidate for soy fortification because doing so will increase its nutritional value and decrease its price. Soy flour is a far less promising candidate because soy fortification will add to the cost of dough while also influencing its consistency, density, and baking properties. The result would be a loss in the dough's usefulness and versatility. These findings suggest that whereas some products are immediately ready for soy fortification, others must be approached carefully.

Example 2: Introducing Soy-Fortified Foods to Colombia

As with Russia, the integration of a new food into Colombia must take into account the people's cultural context and cultural perception of food. However, unlike Russia (which is a lower-context, utilitarian culture),

Colombia is a higher-context, hedonic culture. Colombian people have deep and rich cultural traditions complete with a history of more complex and extravagant foods. To encourage Colombians to accept an unfamiliar food, more attention must be paid to their cultural practices than for Russians. Unlike in Russia, a benefit-oriented communication strategy would be too intrusive in the beginning. Instead, the basic approach of soy fortification would be the most unobtrusive way to introduce soy.

In Colombia, meat is the best candidate for soy fortification because it can be fortified without sacrificing flavor. Specifically, soy-fortified sausages are recommended because some soy fortification is already being done and because fortification will not affect the highly valued taste or texture of the food. Foods such as flour are unacceptable candidates for fortification because adding soy to these products will change the taste in such a way as to make traditional dishes prepared with flour (such as the *arepa*) taste unfamiliar. Only after soy has become integrated into Colombian culture and accepted as a standard ingredient would Colombian chefs be willing to experiment with soy products such as flour. Because integration of a new food product into a higher-context and hedonic culture can come about only as a result of working within the culture, a product that turns familiar products unfamiliar would be undesirable.

Accounting for Culture and Context

If we examine a high–cultural context and hedonic culture such as Colombia we find that cultural traditions play an important role in dictating food consumption behavior. In such a case, soy-fortified meat products would be the best medium to increase soy consumption in that culture. In Russia, soy fortification is also the best initial means to introduce soy into the culture. In a country with a lower cultural context and a utilitarian culture, fortification is the best way to inexpensively improve the nutritional value of Russian foods. Both countries use soy in sausage production, and the conditions are favorable for a further successful integration. If another, less popular product were to be introduced first (such as soy flour), the negative response would make any further soy introductions difficult. When introducing a novel food product, one has to anticipate the introduction of future products because people will be less receptive to additional introductions if their first experience was negative.

Table 13.3 summarizes suggested programs for increasing soy consumption in Russia and Colombia. In general, these suggestions reflect

Table 13.3. Suggested Programs for Increasing Soy Consumption in Russia and Colombia

	Russia ("Lower Context"/Utilitarian)	Colombia ("Higher Context"/Hedonic)
Education and advertising	Direct consumer product advertising, preferably driven by the government, an international agency, or a trusted food organization	• Use indirect product promotions involving publicity • Facilitate word-of-mouth communication beginning with opinion leaders
Product modifications	Integration of soybeans with traditional Russian foods	Find variety of soy food menu items that can provide consumers joy of preparation
Message strategy	• Emphasize the benefits of eating soy (nutrition, cost, flexibility, convenience) • Use factual quantitative advertising • Position soy foods as ordinary, low price foods	• Emphasize the premium and quality aspects of soy foods • Utilize indirect advertising campaigns (e.g., publicity, product placement ads) • Use implicit, dialogue-driven qualitative advertising • Position soy foods as culturally normal, premium foods

Source: Wansink, Sonka, and Cheney (2002).

cultural communication contexts, information needs, and food perception concerns. For the Russian market, we suggest an explicit promotional campaign that highlights the functional and practical aspects of soy, specifically its health and costs benefits. In promoting individual products, care should be taken to position soy foods as simple, efficient, and practical Russian foods that are normal to consume. In the short run, fortifying practical and functional foods (such as ground beef) would allow producers to get a foothold in the market. In the long run, these changes will be widely accepted if they are perceived to increase the utilitarian value of the foods with little cost or inconvenience.

In contrast to Russia, the recommendations for introducing soy into Colombia reflect their higher-context culture and their hedonic perception of food. In the Colombian market, we suggest a more indirect promotional campaign built on publicity, general consumer education programs, and word-of-mouth recommendations from opinion leaders. These methods will be more effective in a higher-context culture in which social bonds and relationships dictate behavior far more profoundly than mass advertising or promotional campaigns. However, unlike the Russian approach (which entails a benefit-focused strategy), the Colombian approach must demonstrate that soy can be used in traditional Colombian foods (such as sausages) while maintaining the traditional rich taste and texture.

Lessons for Marketing Nutrition

Countries with different cultural contexts accept unfamiliar foods in different ways for different reasons. These differences must be reflected in how marketers coordinate product development, promotion campaigns, distribution, and pricing.

Table 13.4 summarizes suggested courses of action according to the cultural context and perception framework. Before one can apply this framework, the country's perception of food (as either hedonic or utilitarian) and its cultural context (low or high) must be assessed. Although this chapter makes broad generalizations about country cultures, different cultural groups or segments coexist in a single country, and our framework must be applied differently to each segment. Once a segment's food perceptions and cultural context have been identified, a marketing campaign should be constructed and executed in line with the suggestions laid out in Table 13.4. For example, for countries with low-context culture and utilitarian perceptions of food, we recommend that marketers emphasize health benefits in a data-driven manner, differentiate these foods as healthful, premium foods, and use direct promotional campaigns to emphasize the personalized benefits of eating these foods.

As noted earlier, the cultural context and perception framework presented here represents a generalization of a population's behavior in a particular culture or country. In every higher-context country there are lower-context subsegments; in every country with a generally hedonic view toward food consumption, there are subsegments with utilitarian views.

The objective of this chapter is not to provide absolute measures for cross-cultural generalizations but to describe a tool that can provide better understanding and insights useful in encouraging the acceptance of unfamiliar foods. Although the scenarios are hypothetical, they illustrate

Table 13.4. Increasing Soy Consumption Using the Cultural Hedonic Framework

Cultural Perception of Food Consumption	Lower Cultural Context	Higher Cultural Context
Hedonic	• Emphasize soy benefits in a data driven and quantitative way • Move to differentiate soy foods as healthy premium foods • Provide accurate, detailed, and complete messages • Use direct consumer product advertising	• Emphasize soy as a cultural, normal, premium food in an implicit, dialogue-driven, and qualitative way • Implement an indirect approach, such as word-of-mouth effects from opinion leaders • Move to differentiate soy foods as premium foods • Use an indirect campaign (e.g., publicity, product placement ads) and facilitate interaction with others • Use general consumer education programs
Utilitarian	• Emphasize the benefits of eating soy foods (e.g., flexibility, convenience) in a data-driven and quantitative way • Move to position soy foods as ordinary, low-priced foods • Emphasize personalized benefits of eating soy • Provide accurate, detailed, and complete message • Use direct consumer product advertising	• Emphasize the benefits of eating soy foods (e.g., flexibility, convenience) in an implicit, dialogue-driven, and qualitative way • Move to position soy foods as ordinary foods, low-priced foods • Implement an indirect approach, such as word-of-mouth effects from opinion leaders or authorized personnel • Use an indirect campaign (e.g., publicity, product placement ads) and facilitate interaction with others • Use general consumer education programs

Source: Wansink, Sonka, and Cheney (2002).

many universal ideas that can be applied to real-life scenarios. Most central is the notion that successful marketing campaigns not only take culture into consideration but also use it as a starting point for integrating a new product. In Colombia and Russia, soy fortification of meat would be a culturally consistent use of soy that offers the best prospects for long-term growth in soy consumption.

This chapter focused on increasing soy consumption in Colombia and Russia. For the purposes of illustration, Figure 13.1 further expands the cultural context and perception framework to include a larger sample of countries based on ratings from more than 227 international consumers. To illustrate within-country variance, the placement of the United States varies depending on whether lower-income or higher-income consumers are considered.

Because this framework reflects broad cultural themes and is not uniquely tied to a country-level analysis, the insights can be applied to other areas in which culture has a significant effect on behavior. With respect to food consumption, possible focal points could include ethnic divisions, social and economic distinctions, geographic boundaries, and

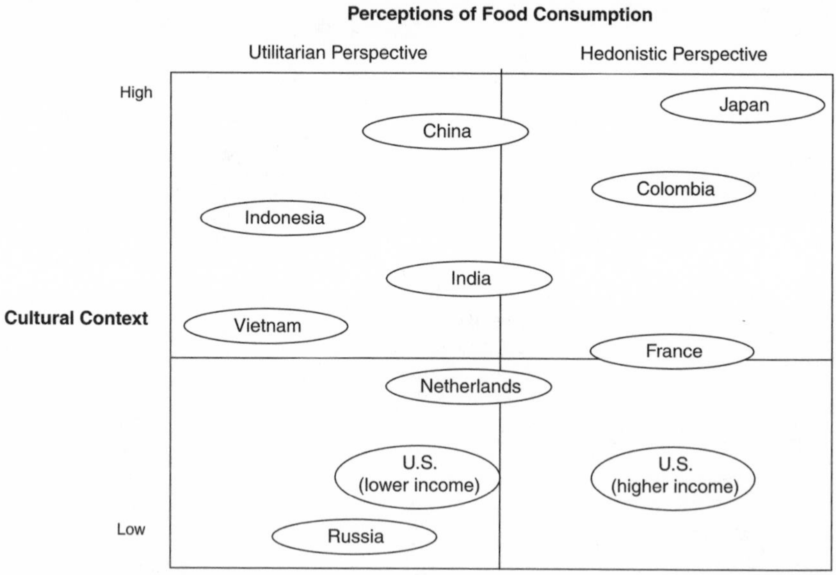

Perceptions of Food Consumption

	Utilitarian Perspective	Hedonistic Perspective

High

China

Japan

Colombia

Indonesia

India

Cultural Context

Vietnam

France

Netherlands

U.S. (lower income)

U.S. (higher income)

Low

Russia

Figure 13.1. Selected countries' locations in the cultural context and perception framework.

psychographic market segments. For instance, an ethnic division study could use this framework to determine how to increase the consumption of tofu among Orthodox Jews or Lent-observing Catholics.

In a more general sense, this research shows us that the cultural context and the utilitarian and hedonic perceptions toward food consumption greatly affect the adoption of unfamiliar foods and behavior. Higher-context societies are more likely to have numerous and complex cultural traditions and practices, which translate into a large number of elaborate cultural food dishes. This can be applied to behavioral processes other than food consumption. For example, studies on athletic involvement, volunteerism, and even political behavior can all be examined using the cultural context and perception framework.

This chapter provided a framework for developing strategies to increase the acceptance of unfamiliar foods. More generally, we explored how culture influences consumption behavior. When developing a marketing strategy around a functional food, it is important to consider cultural context and perceptions. To increase consumption, the marketing strategy must be aligned with the goals and beliefs of the culture. Therefore, it is important to consider all cultural contexts, communications, and product selections when integrating a new marketing program into a culture.

A better understanding of consumer behavior allows us to make marketing decisions based on the consumer insights provided. There is a clear need to assess cultural behaviors and attitudes when carrying out a marketing campaign in a particular culture.

Related Reading

The text for this chapter and the tables and figures in it are adapted from an article previously published in *Review of Agricultural Economics*. The development of recommendations for Russia and Colombia is described in more detail in this article.

Wansink, Brian, Steven T. Sonka, and Matthew M. Cheney. "A Cultural Hedonic Framework for Increasing the Consumption of Unfamiliar Foods: Soy Acceptance in Russia and Colombia." *Review of Agricultural Economics* 24:2 (2002): 353–65.

FOURTEEN

Global Best Practices

Many programs and campaigns to change eating habits have met with costly, disappointing, short-lived results. Most recently, even the adoption of functional foods has been slow because consumers are hesitant to try unfamiliar, initially unappealing foods. The earlier chapters of this book have focused on the insights that have resulted from a stream of research on this topic. Given this framework, this chapter examines a series of best practices from 153 functional food products across the world to provide suggestions that have proven successful in specific situations. They all focus on one basic question: "How can functional foods be incorporated into mainstream diets and long-term eating patterns?"

Given the findings and frameworks that have been described throughout this book, this chapter describes five key themes that we see successfully operating in practice. Each of the examples that is illustrated in the tables of this chapter has helped promote a product. Although in isolation many of these ideas may seem simple, together they point to five central themes that have been effective in promoting products. The specific ideas may not be relevant for every product in every situation, but the basic themes are. In this way, the best practices can be seen as operationalizations or illustrations of a general theme. As such, they provide a starting point for brainstorming.

Each of the illustrations reflects one of the four *P*s of marketing: promotion, price, product, and place. These elements are called the marketing mix because they represent the four levers a marketer can use when trying to encourage a person to buy and consume a particular product. Although the boundary between the four *P*s is not always clear, it provides a convenient way to organize these ideas.

Before describing the five key themes of this chapter, it is important to understand exactly whom these five approaches are targeted at: the food gatekeeper. Doing so will help keep our thinking focused on efforts that are likely to be most efficient.

Focus on Family Gatekeepers

The biggest single driver of consumption is the availability of a particular food. In most households, what is eaten for breakfast, lunch, dinner, and snacks is determined by what the primary grocery shopper—the food gatekeeper—had purchased. As noted in chapter 6, if a teenager wants to eat Pop-Tarts but they are not in the house, his or her chances of eating them are very low. Even though most of us believe that we dictate our own food choices, the options we have are largely determined by whoever does the shopping. Even when we consider what people eat when away from home (be they sack lunches or school lunches), our surveys estimate that around 72 percent of the food decisions by family members are made directly or indirectly by the primary grocery shopper and food preparer.

As underscored throughout this book, this concentration of purchase power and influence is good news for nutrition marketers because it means that we do not have to convince every man, woman, teenager, and child to eat more nutritiously. All we need to do is to convince the food gatekeeper for the family. Convincing the entire country to eat more fruits and vegetables would not be as efficient as simply convincing the primary shopper of the household to buy more fruits and vegetables and fewer processed foods.

Traditionally, the role of gatekeeper has been held almost exclusively by women. However, this trend has shifted. Today, fathers, teenagers, and even preteens are increasingly assuming the role of gatekeepers. This has an important impact on the way companies and agencies should promote functional foods because teenagers are exposed to and influenced by TV or radio advertisements. In addition, children and preteens are gaining influence over purchase decisions because their discretionary time enables them to be more tuned into product innovations and trends.

Five Approaches to Increasing the Consumption of Functional Foods

As noted throughout this book, functional foods have not always been a shopping or consumption priority in our lives. Recall from Figure 7.1 that people order fruits and vegetables much less often than burgers and French fries.

What has been most successful in encouraging people to try and eventually adopt functional foods? We collected case histories of 153 companies (or institutions) from around the world (thirty-one different countries, with the bulk being from the United States) that have successfully marketed functional foods. Each of the best practices was specific to a certain food in a certain environment, but a meta-analysis of these best practices centered around five key themes. Each of these themes is described in this chapter, and some of the best practices associated with them are provided in the accompanying tables. Each practice is categorized based on whether it relates to promoting the product, modifying the product, pricing the product, or placing (distributing) the product.

Increasing Food Availability and Accessibility to Achieve Consumer Awareness

The first common theme is food availability and accessibility. Food availability is the supply of foods from production, imports, or stock. The United States typically enjoys tremendous economic growth and political stability. It is unlikely that there will be any food shortages in the near future, so in this context, increasing food availability entails increasing the availability of functional foods in supermarkets and convenience stores.

One can increase the availability of functional foods by implementing an intensive distribution policy, as Table 14.1 shows. In this way, these products will be available in supermarkets and convenience stores where everyone can find them. Another way to increase availability is by placing functional food products near their counterparts. For example, placing soy-based meat beside the beef would not only contribute to a sense of availability but would also create a perception of substitutability between these two products.

Food availability is complemented by food accessibility. Making sure that functional food products are accessible to consumers is as important as making sure they are available. Accessibility is determined by buying

Table 14.1. Increasing Perception of Functional Food Availability and Accessibility

	Initiative
Product	• Use small packages to induce trial • Sell products in different sizes and forms to allow easy use in any recipe • Make sure the product is easy to prepare and convenient
Price	• Price similar to analog products or slightly higher if targeted to health conscious consumers • Use coupons and discounts to induce trial • When analog product is priced higher, communicate this to consumers
Place	• Use intensive distribution, which is selling though a variety of food retail chains • Use selective distribution, which is placing the product in specific stores such as health stores, specialty food stores, among others • Make agreements with prominent cafeterias and restaurants to use your product • Make agreements to distribute to school and university cafeterias to target health conscious students
Promotions	• Feature the product on cooking shows • Create new uses for the products through recipes and meal ideas • Hold "how to" demos where cooks demonstrate ways to prepare the products onsite and then product samples are delivered • Arrange point of purchase displays that promote the products and its benefits • Use free insert coupons • Use print ads in magazines and newspapers that discuss animal right issues

Source: Adapted from Wansink, Sonka, Chirbogi, Goldsmith, and Eren (2004).

power and price. Because producers and retailers cannot influence buying power directly, they are left to adjust the price. Lower-income families in some countries often cannot regularly afford good cuts of meat. Soy-based products sold as substitutes for red meat could be priced lower. In other words, focusing on the issue of price could enable marketers to make soy-based foods more accessible to the lower-income segment of the market. By communicating to consumers this important product attribute, it is possible to target those who cannot afford higher-priced products.

Increasing Substitutability to Achieve Acceptance

The second theme that applied to many of these best practices is that the marketers succeeded in creating substitutability. Encouraging people to eat functional foods entails replacing the consumption of existing foods with the functional foods. It's not enough to simply encourage someone to purchase a new food; he or she must be convinced to omit something else from his or her diet.

One method used to influence consumers to discontinue the use of a currently favored product is to provide fresh information. For instance, new information about the health benefits of a functional food may cause consumers to reevaluate currently consumed products that lack these health benefits. This is called an interrupt because it causes consumers to interrupt their usual behavior. For example, as a result of Food and Drug Administration regulations concerning soy, it is possible to disclose important information about the health and nutritional benefits of soy and therefore to induce consumers to rethink their purchase decisions.

Even though an interrupt may cause consumers to reconsider their existing consumption habits, it does not necessarily mean that they will modify their purchasing behavior. It means only that they will reconsider their attitudes toward traditional foods. This constitutes an opportunity to promote the health benefits of functional food products that compare favorably to these traditional foods.

A recent study revealed that to encourage cross-category substitution (e.g., substituting fruits for processed foods), it is important to compare the foods by pointing out both similarities and differences. Furthermore, this study revealed that advertising could change consumer attitudes by pointing out differences when the two products are very similar and similarities when the two products are different. Therefore, this approach consists of two main steps: comparing similarities in order to convey a notion of equivalence, and contrasting attributes in order to differentiate the products. In other words, it is important first to show that a functional food can be equivalent to an analog food; once this sense of equivalence becomes salient, it would be wise to point out the attributes that differentiate the products.

Comparing Similarities It is generally understood that most functional foods serve as substitutes for traditional foods. Thus, it is important to create the consumer perception that these foods are equivalent to traditional foods with regard to the attributes that consumers value. For example, people drink soy milk because it contains many of the same nutrients as milk (e.g., calcium). Therefore, people perceive soy milk as a substitute for milk, even though calcium occurs naturally in milk but is added to soy milk.

To convey this sense of substitutability in the mind of consumers, it is important to determine which product attributes must be communicated to the market. One way is to emphasize the nutritional impact of the functional food. By making the nutritional composition of a food product as salient, it is possible to reshape the way consumers compare two products.

Along those same lines, it is also possible to focus on taste and packaging to create a sense of substitutability. For example, the brand Tofutti has a wide range of soy-based frozen desserts that look and taste like traditional frozen desserts. In this case, consumers perceive soy ice cream as a substitute for ice cream because it looks similar and has identical packaging. It is important to note that this is a useful approach only when the taste of the functional food product is similar to that of the traditional food.

Therefore, the objective of this first step is to claim similarities between these two products in order to induce people to seek variety. The next step involves not only a reevaluation of food substitutes but also a change in attitude toward functional foods.

Contrasting Differences   The second step is to contrast both products. Companies should focus not only on the attributes that convey equivalence but also on those that mark the difference. The more similar two products are perceived to be, the more their functional dissimilarities (e.g., soy products' role in preventing heart disease) must be emphasized.

Along those lines, companies could capitalize on the negative consumer perception of certain traditional foods such as red meat and eggs. This can be achieved with the use of advertising and public relations, as seen in Table 14.2. For example, print ads in magazines or articles in newspapers that talk about animal welfare, cattle disease, and other health issues could focus on the functional benefits of eating soy products. As a result, consumers would be induced to position these foods as candidates for substitution because of the functional deficiencies of the analog product.

To conclude, it is critical to position functional food products so that they are perceived as being neither too similar to nor too different from the analog product. Therefore, the main objective is to advertise attributes that will not be made salient simply by the presence of the analog food product.

Table 14.2. Increasing Substitutability of Functional Foods

	Initiatives
Product	• Use attractive packaging similar to analog products • Use nutritional and health benefits on packaging • Position as a healthier food • Label should promote taste by displaying a picture of the product • Labeling should include brand name, ingredients, nutritional facts, best before date, and an endorsement for quality, such as a quality seal • Use different package presentations to target different market segments • Use co-branding with a well-known nonfunctional food brand
Price	• Price similar to analog product • Use coupons or discounts to induce trial
Place	• Place these products near their counterpart in supermarkets and convenience stores • Introduce an incentive program to motivate retailers to carry these products
Promotions	• When advertising place emphasis on good taste similar to that of analog product • Use joint promotions with a well-known nonfunctional food to induce familiarity • Include a picture of the product in the advertisement and real-life product endorsements to give consumers a more vivid feeling of the product • Feature the product on a cooking show where both classic and exotic dishes will be prepared step-by-step • Use reliable, well-liked, and fit models or TV stars as a spokesperson for your product

Using Alternative Frames of Reference to Increase Preference

The first step in making a decision is to frame it as a question, such as, "Should I eat this functional food?" The way a problem or question is framed influences the choices people make. People often find themselves in conflict because opposing forces that induce them to act in different ways under the same circumstances. Driving forces are those that help people move toward a desired state or perform a desired activity. For example, consumers buy tofu because of its nutritional benefits. Restraining forces are those that motivate people to move away from an undesired goal. For example, consumers who enjoy red meat don't purchase tofu because of its perceived bad taste. Conflict occurs when a person confronts two opposite forces. For example, conflict occurs when consumers are willing to try tofu because of its nutritional benefits but avoid purchasing it because of its taste.

Consumers face conflict with functional food consumption because a driving force induces them to try these foods. This force usually takes the form of health benefits for the consumer. In the same way, consumers face a restraining force that induces them not to try these foods. This force generally takes the form of less pleasant taste. As seen in Table 14.3, it is important to use advertising and promotions to place greater emphasis on driving forces such as nutrition and health. The goal then becomes educating and motivating consumers to use health and nutritional issues as a frame of reference that will help them decide which food to purchase in the future.

A prominent decision-making study revealed that people are risk averse when a problem is posed to them in terms of gains but risk seeking when the problem is framed in terms of losses. It is possible to capitalize on these results by framing the information presented to consumers in a way that suggests product trial and consumption. Consumers perceive buying healthful products as a decision that involves risk. In this case, the risk consists of buying the healthful product and not liking the product's

Table 14.3. Changing the Frames of Reference

	Initiatives
Product	• Use recyclable package to promote consumer goodwill • Position the foods as healthier • Nutritional information should be prominently displayed with facts (e.g., lack of cholesterol or fat) highlighted • Segment product according to consumers view of food (i.e., healthy vs. pleasure)
Price	• In general terms, price similar to analog products
Place	• Use selective distribution to target specialty stores, health stores, nutrition clubs • Place these foods near their nonsoy counterpart in supermarkets
Promotions	• Sponsor a governmental agency that promotes health and nutritious eating • Place handouts, triptychs, or leaflets in health and fitness clubs • Sponsor health and nutrition agencies • Use cross-marketing with another food product that is health-oriented • Use guilt factor by discussing in newspaper and magazine articles and ads the health problems caused by traditionally unhealthy foods

Source: Adapted from Wansink, Sonka, Chirbogi, Goldsmith, and Eren (2004).

taste. The key is to achieve trial and acceptance by framing the information presented to consumers in such a way that potential losses for not consuming healthful foods are discussed. For example, Table 14.3 notes advertising the potential health problems caused by traditional foods instead of describing the nutritional benefits of functional foods. The possible losses are emphasized rather than the gains from eating well. This sidesteps the perceived risk from purchasing healthful products: bad taste.

Using Group Commitment to Increase Consumption

The previous section discussed the conflict that arises from driving and restraining forces, but conflict also occurs when the needs of the individual conflict with the needs of the group. This is particularly important when the individual has a strong sense of belonging to the group or to a particular ethnic, religious, or social identity. When an individual succumbs to the goals of the group because of a desire to belong, it is said that these external forces have induced him or her to maintain the status quo of the group. Therefore, these forces are called induced forces.

It is possible to use these induced forces to promote functional food consumption. The goal is to motivate a group to consume more healthful products based on a group principle or value. Table 14.4 mentions that one such principle or value could be a responsibility to eat well. The group transmits these principles to new group members, thus influencing them to try more healthful, functional foods. For example, if people at a health club generally drink fortified juices, a newcomer to the club may consider or even feel compelled to try them. Therefore, it is important to promote functional food consumption through social groups, formal or informal.

A group decision is more effective when it is approached as a way to involve people who would usually avoid functional foods. A group decision method used to change food habits is more effective than a lecture method. If individuals are involved in the group's decision, they will be more likely to accept the product more readily. The reason is that they feel committed to the ultimate decision because they were part of the decision process and share a sense of belonging to the group. Then, their sense of responsibility to eat well motivates them to favor healthful foods.

Changing the Salience of Consumer Beliefs

The last approach involves changing the way consumers think about functional foods. As a preliminary step, it is necessary to position these

Table 14.4. Increasing Functional Food Consumption through the
Commitment of the Group

	Initiatives
Product	• Display charitable contribution in the packaging • Segment product according to family size • Use warm family images in packaging • Use cartoon characters or famous TV program stars in the packaging to evoke familiarity and a sense of fun
Price	• Use discounts for consumers who purchase larger family-sized packages • Use coupons and discounts temporarily during special holidays such as Father's Day or Mother's Day
Place	• Make agreements to sell product in health and nutrition clubs, fitness centers, social groups
Promotions	• Sponsor a philanthropic event. Celebrities are good spokespersons for this type of promotion. • Set up a tent at a popular city festival where product information, as well as free samples, could be distributed to attendees • Sponsor school activities where children could learn more about the particular functional food and its benefits and give away samples of the product • Donate a percentage of profits to charities that are important to that culture • Use public relations in the form of third-party articles that discuss the responsibility of eating healthy • Use advertising that depicts a happy family that eats healthy

foods as socially acceptable products in order to induce consumption. One method of achieving this is by creating consumer perceptions of functional foods as increasing social status.

Certain foods serve as symbols of a family's social status. A household that stops consuming red meat for reasons other than vegetarianism is considered to have lost social status. Therefore, families in the middle- to upper-income segment of the market usually continue to purchase foods such as red meat regardless of price increases. Lower-income families will be reluctant to discontinue the purchase of foods such as red meat unless there is a less expensive substitute that renders the same status.

According to Table 14.5, companies can induce consumers to perceive a functional food as having the same social status as traditional foods by pricing them as high as or higher than traditional foods or using another cue such as an attractive packaging. For example, this strategy can work with soy substitutes for meat. When less price-sensitive consumers see that these substitutes cost the same as red meat, they will assign them the

Table 14.5. Changing the Salience of Consumer Beliefs

	Initiatives
Product	• Position the food as a healthy food with nutritional benefits and good taste • Use bright colors and eye-catching logos in packaging • Nutritional information should be prominently displayed with facts about lack of cholesterol and fat highlighted • Use green colors in packaging to evoke health and nature • Use product-specific colors, like golden colors, in the packaging to evoke the soy plant, for example • Use catchy product-specific slogans such as "Here is to soy, here is to life" and "Love your family, think soy" • Product brand name should usually evoke health
Price	• Use price as a symbol of social status (charge premium) for those functional foods that substitute traditional foods with such social status
Place	• Use incentive programs to target restaurants and cafeterias • Place functional foods near their counterpart
Promotions	• Use marketing research in the form of surveys and focus group to find out the consumer perception of the particular functional food • Use a series of TV ads to educate and promote your product to the public • Focus on guilt-free feeling as a result of eating as much as you want and still feeling healthy • Use consumer's guilt factor, perhaps by discussing animal rights issues or the issues of eating unhealthy • When using advertising, use same values as your target segment (i.e., self-fulfillment)

same social status because they use price as a measure of value. However, companies can also decide to price lower and use attractive packaging to induce substitution from lower-income people. In short, companies can choose to price lower or higher in order to target different market segments. Both strategies can coexist if a company uses separate brands as a way to segment the market effectively.

It is also possible to use other social endorsements such as modeling to portray functional foods as foods that should be accepted readily in every family's kitchen. Consumers tend to buy image-oriented products that are either consistent with their positive view of themselves, or consistent with their aspirations. People tend to project their images onto famous figures, so if a celebrity consumes and favors functional food products, it is more likely that consumers will do so as part of the image they want to project to the people around them.

Advertising and promotions make it possible to change consumers' perceptions with regard to functional foods, positioning them as tasting good and conveying high social status. To do so, it is necessary to change consumers' attitudes toward functional foods. Consumer behavior theory establishes three strategies to modify the attitudes of consumers.

Add a New Salient Belief   This could be achieved by focusing on new attributes of the product. For example, eating soy-based foods provides protein and prevents heart disease. Adding utilitarian attributes such as health benefits has a greater effect on the individual than hedonistic attributes such as better taste. It is possible to influence consumers to see this utilitarian benefit as a salient attribute. As seen in Table 14.5, it is effective to list such benefits on the product's package.

Change the Evaluation of an Existing Belief   This entails changing the way consumers evaluate traditional foods. Consumers evaluate these foods primarily using hedonistic criteria such as taste and presentation. By using techniques such as modeling, marketers can redefine the way consumers evaluate functional food products. For example, a famous athlete could be hired to discuss the disadvantages of eating fried foods compared to fruits and vegetables in a series of TV ads.

In addition, Table 14.5 shows that it is effective to lure consumers away from traditional foods such as meat or vegetable oil by discussing price issues or the consequences of consuming such products, such as high cholesterol levels and animal welfare issues. The idea is to influence consumers to de-emphasize taste as an attribute. If there is more guilt associated with choosing a hedonic attribute, hedonic attributes may be less important in acquisition choices.

Make an Existing Belief More Salient   Marketers can increase the salience of an attribute by promoting the benefits of eating well and thereby inducing consumers to use nutrition as a primary criterion in deciding which food to purchase. This entails focusing even further on the benefits of eating well (e.g., feeling energetic). The goal is to induce consumers to place higher emphasis on motivators such as health issues and therefore consider them another important attribute to check when purchasing food.

As seen in Table 14.5, there are different ways to change consumers' attitudes and behavior toward functional foods. It is important to communicate the desired attributes to best position these foods as a substitute for traditional foods and to de-emphasize the attributes that prove detrimental.

Lessons for Marketing Nutrition

Best practices from 153 different global marketers of functional foods revealed five useful approaches that can be used to change previous attitudes that people held with respect to healthful eating. These include increasing the availability of functional foods, increasing the substitutability of functional foods, using alternative frames of reference, using group decisions as a way to reach a commitment to try healthful foods, and changing the salience of consumer beliefs. Various elements of the best practices described in this chapter can be adapted to any food or marketing situation.

Past efforts have focused on all consumers. The first part of this chapter underscored the importance of focusing scarce marketing dollars and energy on the family gatekeeper and not on all family members. If the gatekeeper in a family directly or indirectly makes more than 72 percent of the food-related decisions, that should be where marketing efforts are directed. Chapter 6 described what these gatekeepers look like and which ones can be targeted most effectively.

Related Readings

A more comprehensive treatment of these issues can be found in the following article.

Wansink, B., S. Sonka, P. Goldsmith, J. Chiriboga, and N. Eren. "Increasing Acceptance of Soy-based Foods," *Journal of International Food and Agribusiness Marketing* 16:1, forthcoming.

Conclusion: Looking Backward and Speeding Forward

As the Introduction to this book emphasized, marketing nutrition is not simply a clever "Got Milk" ad, a fifty-cent coupon on a soy burger, or a convenient combination pack of precut carrots. In the context of nutrition, marketing is much broader because it focuses on all efforts to persuade, encourage, and enable people to eat more nutritiously. Call it education, public service, or simply good parenting. Sometimes it takes the form of education programs or innovative distribution programs, and sometimes it takes the form of more direct efforts. Marketing involves determining how to help a patient eat a lower-fat diet, encourage a hungry family to eat protein-rich grains, help a shopper understand a health label, or encourage a child to finish his or her vegetables.

If food is so central to health, why aren't we more successful in altering behavior? Part of this difficulty can be attributed to some of the well-meaning but misguided perspectives that are brought to the marketing of nutrition. These efforts often are directed by talented people who have the right intentions but the wrong experiences. This book began with four common but misguided perspectives of four hypothetical people: a dietitian, a government administrator, a marketing manager, and a researcher. Let's revisit these perspectives and then see how things might have changed (Table C.1).

Dietitians and Health Care Professionals

Consider the notion that nutritional knowledge is power. Sometimes it is assumed that once people know that food is nutritious, they will consume it. Too much day-to-day contact with highly salient nutritional knowledge may lead some well-meaning nutrition experts and dietitians to believe that simply passing on this knowledge will induce change. As noted earlier, these efforts have been generally unsuccessful in the same way that knowing that doing fifty situps every morning is good for us does

Table C.1. Speeding Forward and Changing Perspectives

	Perspective	
Profession	Backward-Looking	Forward-Looking
Dieticians and healthcare professionals	Nutritional knowledge is power	Understand taste, then understand nutrition
Public policy officials and food aid administrators	Food aid is food eaten	Persuade, then provide
Brand managers	Marketing nutrition is like marketing soap	Half taste, half perception
Researchers and academics	Here's the data	Rigor and relevance

not motivate many of us to do it. Unfortunately, many people will not eat better even if we can get them to pass a nutrition quiz.

A new and better approach is to understand taste, then nutrition. A good dietitian or health care professional understands that nutrition education will solve nutrition problems only when it's relevant to one's personal circumstances and appealing to one's individual tastes.

An important lesson for these professionals is that different people have different predispositions to different foods. Knowing a person's taste profile will help an effective dietitian design a nutrition plan and a nutritional message that will be heard. For instance, fruit lovers tend to prefer sweet snacks, so it is best to encourage them to eat fruit snacks instead of cookies. Rather than trying to change everyone's behavior, realize that some people are more likely to change their eating behaviors than others. By developing profile clusters of ideal consumers and by discovering why people like the foods they like, an effective dietitian can find similarly predisposed people and help them develop the same mental map for that food.

One key step to understanding taste is being able to estimate a person's likelihood of adopting a food before actually trying to change his or her diet. One way to do this is to determine the person's cultural flexibility and whether he or she views food as functional or hedonic. When nutritional knowledge is involved, it is important to keep it simple. For probably 90 percent of the world, simple health messages are best (recall the health claims in chapter 12). The rest of the consumers will seek out the details in their own time. In general, nutritional messages are most effective when you target a specific population with a quantitative but personal message.

Although understanding tastes is important, tastes can also be subtly influenced. Unappealing names (e.g., *soy* and *gooseberry*) can make for unappealing tastes. Simply using creative and descriptive names can improve the acceptance and taste of foods. Finally, never underestimate the influence of a good cook. These cooks largely determine the eating habits of the family. Change the habits of the cook and you will directly or indirectly change many of the eating habits of the family. Good cooks are the nutritional gatekeepers of the home, and they account for more than 70 percent of the food consumption decisions in a household.

Public Policy Officials

The basic perspective that food aid is food eaten was very relevant to the post–World War I Hoover Administration. This is predicated on the notion that distressed people resort to desperate measures. Although this is true under extreme circumstances, the issue today usually is not whether people will get enough calories but whether they'll get the right calories. The "food aid is food eaten" assumption does not apply to people who can elect to consume food that tastes better but is much less nutritionally dense.

Instead of shipping and dumping food, a new and better approach should be to persuade, then provide. If the key to malnutrition today is less the amount of food eaten and more the types of food eaten, part of what policy officials and food aid administrators have to know is that they must persuade first and then provide. International food aid efforts will be most successful when they match the cultural flexibility and food views of a population. Although nutritional knowledge is important, it is not sufficient for behavior change. Science doesn't sell, and people don't necessarily want to be informed of the details unless there are notable risks involved.

One of the more sensitive issues for public policy officials involves food scares. In these cases, the risks of the unknown are more important than benefits. Even if attitudes can be changed about the risks of biotechnology, people will avoid risks long before they see the benefits of biotechnology. Chapter 10 offers suggestions on how to manage reactions through proactive precrisis preparations and crisis-related responses.

The notion of persuading and then providing is also a key to the success of programs such as the Five-a-Day program. In this case, many people appear to have a natural preference for either fruits or vegetables. As a result, message strategies and targeting should be based on taste profiles and on making substitutions for favored foods. Programs will be most effective if they induce quick change in a predisposed group. Profiling ideal consumers reveals that people are not blank slates; they have mental maps of foods. These mental maps indicate who will be most likely to adopt a food and why.

What types of health claims are most effective? Put complete health claims on the back of packages and short claims on the front. In general, the most effective health claims have some critical common elements. They target a specific segment, receive a great deal of media attention, highlight quantitative health benefits, and address personal health problems.

Research also shows that names are important. Although they are the same food, Kiwi fruit sells; prickly pears don't. A name should accurately represent a product but give it a fighting chance in the market. Descriptive names must truthfully represent a product. If they don't, they can compromise a producer's credibility and can even be harmful to those with allergies.

Brand Managers

A third misconception is that marketing nutrition is the same as marketing any other attribute of a product, whether it's fluoride for toothpaste, passenger-side airbags for cars, or a fresh scent in a detergent. As noted earlier, food is a very different venue from the more rational contexts of toothpaste and car shopping. Everyone is an expert with foods: we all know what we like. Yet the marketing of nutritious foods must delicately balance emotion with reason. Convincing someone to eat soy because it may help reduce weight will be unsuccessful if consumers see it as a magic pill that will eliminate health problems or if they see it as something they have to tolerate—like medicine—a couple of times before returning to a diet of hamburger.

The better approach can be expressed as "half taste, half perception." This is based on the notion that there are some consumer variables that can be controlled, and there are others that cannot. We can change people's tastes only to a small degree, but we find the people whose tastes are most in line with our intentions toward the target food, even if they currently don't eat this target food.

Many marketing managers have prematurely—and wrongly—celebrated the awarding of a health claim, thinking it would solve all marketing woes. Health claims are not silver bullets. Sometimes they can help, such as when a marketer uses both sides of a package to communicate health claims (short on front and long on back). Indeed, the most successful health claims are those that have been carefully targeted and copromoted. They have also been specific, quantitative, and personal in their message.

The value of open communication also applies to issues that could backfire, including biotechnology. Although it might hibernate, the biotech controversy will not fade away. It is important to realize that honest communication about biotechnology is not just a trade association issue, it is also a company imperative. Efforts should focus on non–risk-averse consumers, being specific about the risks associated with certain foods.

Half of the marketing equation is focused on taste. Instead of being targeted only on the basis of demographic dimensions, people should be targeted on the basis of their taste profiles. For instance, fruit is preferred by sweet snack lovers, and vegetables are preferred by cooking enthusiasts. Profiling can be used to segment consumers into groups based on their predispositions. Focus groups do not show the true picture. Mental maps of food champions show the ideal associations that must be developed to convert nonbelievers. Similarly, when food operations are being expanded overseas, a modified cultural context and perception framework can be used to help prioritize countries and cultures based on their adoption likelihood.

Although it is easier to target tastes than to change them, there is some opportunity to help consumers learn to like new tastes. People can be fairly suggestible when it comes to food names. If the name sounds bad, it will bias taste. As long as a food is of at least moderate quality, the better the description, the better the taste.

In general, however, when trying to encourage changes in habits, it is easier to encourage small, infrequent substitutions when introducing new foods. It is also easier to target opinion leaders and nutritional gatekeepers than to target everyone. Good cooks have a tremendous influence over the eating behaviors of their families. If they buy it, it stands a good chance of being eaten.

Scientists and Researchers

The distracting multiple-project life of active researchers leads them to develop a perspective best characterized as "Here are the results; my work is done." Although it may help maximize the number of projects one completes, this attitude does not maximize the impact of any one project.

Increasingly, the more successful grant-getters and accolade winners are those who combine research and relevance. They are scientists whose work receives the respect of their peers *and* has an impact on practice. What this means is that one cannot simply deliver the data and leave. Instead, one must make certain that it is disseminated in an easily understandable way through the media or through papers that are widely available. Also, it increasingly means that academics must develop partnerships with social scientists who focus on consumer adoption or professionals who specialize in implementation. Simply being a biochemistry expert isn't enough anymore.

Not all consumers are alike. Research participants should be segmented based on taste predispositions. For instance, don't expect sweet snack lovers to effectively taste test vegetables. Innovators and opinion leaders should be treated differently because they are different. They necessitate diverse types of information and various levels of attention.

The real reasons behind preferences and behavior cannot be captured in a sociological questionnaire. Laddering and mental mapping should precede any quantitative efforts. So should a review of earlier research related to a topic. If it's important, it's been attempted before.

Not surprisingly, all four of these perspectives are commonly observed in nutrition marketing. As noted earlier, dietitians and scientists are well versed in the science behind the food, not in the acceptance of the foods. Government officials working with food aid often are experts in logistics and project management, not in consumer acceptance or compliance. Brand managers who find themselves working with health foods (perhaps as part of a two-year rotation) are experts in marketing, price promotions, and advertising for popular brands of soap and cereal. They are less familiar with a product that has little or no established following and often necessitates a trade-off between health benefits and the more easily promoted hedonic ones.

Final Lessons for Marketing Nutrition

Each reader should get something different out of the material presented here, which is summarized in Table C.2.

Throughout these chapters I have discussed a wide variety of products and contexts. The subtitle of this book—"Soy, Functional Foods, Biotechnology, and Obesity"—notes four areas in which marketing nutrition has become important and visible. Although I have made specific references

Table C.2. Marketing Nutrition Take-aways for Four Groups of Thought Leaders

	Dieticians and Healthcare Professionals	Administrators of Food Aid Programs and Public Policy Officials	Brand Managers	Scientists and Researchers
1. Nutrition education that matters	• Don't insist that nutrition education will solve nutrition problems. •Emphasize the attributes of foods *and* the personal benefits of eating them.	• Understand that while nutritional knowledge is important, if it not sufficient for behavior change. • Science doesn't sell.	• Health claims are not "Silver Bullets" that make everything better. Continue to rely on basic marketing tools.	• Biochemistry isn't enough. • Research programs to improve health must examine behavior change and not only knowledge acquisition.
2. Classified World War II secrets	• Remember that accepted foods are SAFE: Selected, Available, Familiar, and Exactly as expected.	• Research conducted long ago can still have immense value today. Many food problems don't change that much.	• Encourage small, infrequent substitutions to introduce new foods into diets.	• Don't neglect "old" and unpublished research when starting a new topic. • If it's important, it's been attempted before.
3. If it sounds good, it tastes good	• Unappealing names make for unappealing tastes. • Use creative and descriptive names to improve the acceptance and taste of foods.	• Kiwi fruit sells, prickly pears don't. • Names should accurately give products a fighting chance. • Be careful that descriptive names truthfully represent a product.	• If the name sounds bad, it will bias taste. Change it. • As long as a food is at least of moderate quality, the better the description, the better the taste.	• The names in experiments can bias taste. Leave them out of the equation when possible. • In taste tests, people taste what they think they are going to taste.

Table C.2. Cont.

	Dieticians and Healthcare Professionals	Administrators of Food Aid Programs and Public Policy Officials	Brand Managers	Scientists and Researchers
4. Profiling the perfect consumer	• Specific profiles of people are more likely to change eating behaviors than others. • Develop profile clusters of ideal consumers and seek out others with similar traits.	• Programs will be most effective and encouraging if they encourage quick change among a predisposed group. • Use this method to profile ideal consumers for specific foods.	• Profiling can be used to segment consumers into groups based on their predispositions. • Personality traits can be better than demographics.	• Not all people should be treated the same. • Innovators and opinion leaders should be treated differently because they are different.
5. Mental maps that lead to consumer insights	• Discover why people who like a food really like that food. • Try to develop the same mental map for that food in others.	• People are not blank slates—they have mental maps of foods. • Developing mental maps indicates who will be most likely to adopt a food and why.	• Mental maps of food champions show the ideal associations that need to be developed in nonbelievers. • Focus groups do not show the true picture.	• The real reasons behind preferences and behavior cannot be captured in a questionnaire. • Laddering and mental mapping should preceed any quantitative efforts.
6. Targeting nutritional gatekeepers	• Good cooks largely determine the eating habits of the family. • Target the three most influential types of good cooks.	• To change eating habits, target the cooks, not the consumers.	• There are three types of good cooks who lead trends and opinions.	• Personalities differentiate good cooks better than behavior or food usage.

Table C.2. Cont.

	Dieticians and Healthcare Professionals	Administrators of Food Aid Programs and Public Policy Officials	Brand Managers	Scientists and Researchers
7. The De-marketing of obesity	• Small daily changes in intake (50-100 calories) will arrest the obesity problem in 90 percent of Americans. • Help clients alter the availability, convenience, and variety of foods in their homes.	• People want variety, value, and convenience, and this needs always to be kept in mind. • Labeling and instructions are good but are likely to have a small impact.	• People want variety, value, and convenience. Always provide alternatives. • Label products as visibly as possible.	• Investigate how interventions related to the ten drivers of consumption will most influence intake.
8. Why five-a-day programs often fail	• Many people are either more predisposed to fruits or to vegetables. Encourage people to consume the one they're most likely to consume. • Fruit lovers tend toward sweet snacks. Encourage fruit snacks instead.	• People have natural leanings toward either fruits or vegetables. This needs to be taken into account for Five-a-Day programs to work. • Message strategies and targeting should be based on taste profiles and on making substitutions for favored foods.	• Target people based on their taste profiles. • Fruit consumption is correlated with sweet snack consumption. • Vegetables are preferred by cooking enthusiasts.	• Not all consumers are alike. People and taste panelists should be segmented based on taste predispositions. • Don't expect sweet snack lovers to effectively taste test vegetables.

Table C.2. Cont.

	Dieticians and Healthcare Professionals	Administrators of Food Aid Programs and Public Policy Officials	Brand Managers	Scientists and Researchers
9. Winning the biotechnology battle	• People learn information both directly and indirectly. • Changing attitude does not change behavior if emotion is involved.	• People don't necessarily want to be informed of the details. • Risks of the unknown are more important than benefits. • Changing attitudes does not change behavior.	• Although it might hibernate, the biotech controversy will not fade away. • What's good for medicine is not necessarily good for food.	• Knowing the facts will not change people's mind if emotion is involved.
10. Managing consumer reactions to food crises	• You can change risk perceptions, but you can't change risk attitudes.	• Honest, clear information about risks (and risk percentages) can change perceptions. • Panic can be reduced by focusing on non–risk-averse consumers.	• Focus efforts on non-risk-averse consumers. • Be specific about the riskiness of foods (use risk percentages).	• Modeling risk reactions must include the interaction between both risk perceptions and risk attitudes.
11. Leveraging FDA health claims	• Claims are most effective when you target a specific relevant population with a quantitative but personal message.	• Effective claims target a specific segment, receive much media attention, highlight quantitative health benefits, and address personal health problems.	• Target, copromote, and be specific, quantitative, and personal in the message.	• Health claims are only beneficial if understood and adopted by consumers.

Table C.2. Cont.

	Dieticians and Healthcare Professionals	Administrators of Food Aid Programs and Public Policy Officials	Brand Managers	Scientists and Researchers
12. Health claims—when less equals more?	• Keep it simple. For 90 percent of the world, simple health messages are best. The rest will seek out the details.	• Put complete health claims on the back of packages and short claims on the front.	• Use both sides of a package to communicate health claims—short on front, long on back.	• Most people are uninvolved, simplified information processors. They ignore the details.
13. Introducing unfamiliar foods to unfamiliar lands	• Assess a person's likelihood for adoption before trying to change their diet. • To do this, determine their cultural flexibility and whether they view food as functional or hedonic.	• Food aid and relief efforts will be most successful when they match the cultural flexibility and food views of a culture. • Consider likelihood of success when prioritizing cultures.	• You don't sell beef to India or pork to Israel. • When expanding food operations overseas, this framework will help prioritize countries and cultures based on their adoption likelihood.	• Use the cultural flexibility and food perceptions dimension of the cultural hedonic framework in cross-cultural research.
14. Global best practices	• Focus on encouraging healthy food substitutions by focusing on what they get, not what they are avoiding. • Position healthy foods as socially acceptable mainstream foods, not as fringe foods.	• Availability and accessibility are the dominate drivers of consumption. Make sure healthy alternatives are available. • Positive reasons to try a healthy food are more effective than negative reasons to avoid an unhealthy one.	• Increase food availability and accessibility to achieve awareness. • Increase substitutability to achieve acceptance. • Use new frames of reference to enhance preference. • Use group commitment to increase consumption. • Change the salience of beliefs.	• Realize that every action entails a reaction that must be accounted for; eating one food typically means foregoing another. • Try to anticipate unintended consequences of seemingly healthy changes in dietary behavior.

to each throughout the book, the general principles are germane to each. As noted in the Introduction, the challenge in marketing nutrition is not in reinventing the wheel. Lessons from previous failures and successes can be applied to other contexts to encourage better nutrition. The same tools and insights that have helped make less nutritious products popular can also be used to bring people back to a more healthful lifestyle.

It has been said that the nineteenth century was the century of hygiene. That is, in the nineteenth century more lives were saved or extended through an improved understanding of hygiene (germs, infection, etc.) than through any other single development. The twentieth century could reasonably be called the century of medicine. Medicine was responsible for saving and extending lives as never before. At the close of century, the average lifespan of Americans was more than seventy-five years. Although fundamental medical discoveries remain that will extend lives, at this point many of the changes that will further contribute most to extending and adding quality to people's lives are based on behavioral changes. They entail reducing risky behavior and improving exercise and nutrition.

At this point medicine may be less influential in extending our lifespan and our quality of life than the behavioral changes that effective marketing efforts can encourage. Smart, responsible marketers may be best suited to effectively lead this movement. Nutrition is a good place to start.

References and Suggested Readings

Aaron, J. I., R. E. Evans, and D. J. Mela. "Paradoxical Effect of a Nutrition Labeling Scheme in a Student Cafeteria." *Nutrition Research* 15:9 (1995): 1251–61.

Abbott, A. "BSE Fallout Sends Shock Waves through Germany." *Nature* 409 (January 2001): 275.

Ajzen, I. "The Theory of Planned Behavior." *Organizational Performance and Human Decision Processes* 50 (1991): 179–211.

Aldhous, P. "Inquiry Blames Missed Warnings for Scale of Britain's BSE Crisis." *Nature* 408 (November 2000): 3–5.

Barnes, S. "Evolution of the Health Benefits of Soy Isoflavones." *Proceedings of the Society for Experimental Biology and Medicine* 217:3 (1998): 386–92.

Bartholomew, R. E., and E. Goode. "Mass Delusions and Hysterias, Highlights from the Past Millennium." *Skeptical Inquirer* 24:3 (May/June 2000).

Blumer, H. "Outline of Collective Behavior." In *Readings in Collective Behavior*. E. Robert R. Evans. 65–88. Chicago: Rand McNally, 1969.

Bollman, M. "Influence of Food Preparation Methods on Acceptance in the Army," *Second Session: Food Preparation and Serving Methods and Their Relation to Food Habits and Nutrition*. Chicago: Quartermaster Food and Container Institute for the Armed Forces, 1945.

Borre, O. "Public Opinion on Gene Technology in Denmark 1987 to 1989." *Biotech Forum Europe* 7 (1990): 471–77.

Bredahl, L., K. G. Grunert, and L. J. Frewer. "Consumer Attitudes and Decision-Making with Regard to Genetically Engineered Food Products: A Review of the Literature and a Presentation of Models for Future Research." *Journal of Consumer Policy* 21 (1998): 251–77.

Cardello, A. V. "Consumer Expectations and Their Role in Food Acceptance." In *Measurement of Food Preferences*. Ed. H. J. MacFie and D. M. H. Thomson. 253–97. London: Blackie Academic, 1994.

Cardello, A. V., O. Maller, H. B. Masor, C. Dubose, and B. Edelman. "Role of Consumer Expectancies in the Acceptance of Novel Foods." *Journal of Food Science* 50:6 (1985): 1707.

Cardello, A. V., and F. M. Sawyer. "Effects of Disconfirmed Consumer Expectations on Food Acceptability." *Journal of Sensory Studies* 7 (1992): 253–77.

Cardello, A. V., H. Schutz, C. Snow, and L. Lesher. "Predictors of Food Acceptance, Consumption and Satisfaction in Specific Eating Situations." *Food Quality and Preference* 11:3 (2000): 201–16.

Caswell, J. A., and E. M. Mojduszka. "Using Informational Labeling to Influence the Market for Quality in Food Products." *American Journal of Agricultural Economics* 78:5 (1996): 1248–53.

Chandon, P., and B. Wansink. "When Are Stockpiled Products Consumed Faster? A Convenience-Salience Framework of Post-purchase Consumption Incidence and Quantity." *Journal of Marketing Research* 39:3 (August 2002): 321–35.

Chandon, P., B. Wansink, and G. Laurent. "A Benefit Congruency Framework of Sales Promotion Effectiveness." *Journal of Marketing* 64 (October 2000): 65–81.

Christensen, L., and L. Pettijohn. "Mood and Carbohydrate Cravings." *Appetite* 36:2 (2001): 137–45.

Coletta, F. A. "Road Map for Functional Foods: Central Challenge and Major Priorities." *Nutrition Today* 34:4 (1999): 166–69.

Cummings, R. O. "Historical Influences and Regional Differences in the United States Food Habits." *Fifth Session: Regional vs. National Food Habits and Nutrition,* Committee on Food Habits (mimeographed), 1945.

Dake, K. "Orientating Dispositions in the Perception of Risk: An Analysis of Contemporary Worldviews and Cultural Biases." *Journal of Cross-Cultural Psychology* 22 (1991): 61–82.

Daria, I. *Lutèce: A Day in the Life of America's Greatest Restaurant.* New York: Random House, 1993.

Decker, K. J. "The Dominant Culture: Yogurt for the Masses." *Food Product Design* (April 2001).

Deliza, R., and H. J. H. MacFie. "The Generation of Sensory Expectation by External Cues and Its Effect on Sensory Perception and Hedonic Ratings: A Review." *Journal of Sensory Studies* 11:2 (1996): 103–28.

Dickins, D. "A Regional Approach to Food Habits and Attitude Research," *Second Session: Food Preparation and Serving Methods and Their Relation to Food Habits and Nutrition,* Committee on Food Habits (mimeographed), 1945.

Doyle, M. *The Consumer Research Report.* 31:1 (2000): 3.

Drewnoski, A., S. A. Henderson, C. S. Hann, W. A. Berg, and M. T. Ruffin, "Genetic Taste Markers and Preferences for Vegetables and Fruit of Female Breast Care Patients." *Journal of the American Dietetic Association,* 100 (Feb. 2, 2000): 191–97.

Ekos Research Associates Inc. *Biotechnology Research Design, Final Report.* Ottawa: Industry Canada, 1995.

Ekos Research Associates Inc. *Focus Groups on Agri-Food Applications of Biotechnology. Summary Report.* Ottawa: Industry Canada, 1996.

Fischhoff, B., P. Slovic, S. Lichtenstein, S. Read, and B. Combs. "How Safe Is Safe Enough? A Psychometric Study of Attitudes towards Technological Risks and Benefits." *Policy Sciences* 9 (1978): 127–52.

Fishbein, M., and I. Ajzen. *Belief, Attitude, Intention and Behavior: An Introduction to Theory and Research.* Reading, Mass.: Addison-Wesley, 1975.

Food Marketing Institute. "Trends in American Eating Patterns 2002," Washington, D.C.: Food Marketing Institute, 2002.

Frewer, L. J., D. Hedderley, C. Howard, and R. Shepherd. "'Objection' Mapping in Determining Group and Individual Concerns Regarding Genetic Engineering." *Agriculture and Human Values* 14 (1997): 67–79.

Frewer, L. J., C. Howard, D. Hedderley, and R. Shepherd. "What Determines Trust in Information about Food-Related Risks? Underlying Psychological Constructs." *Risk Analysis* 16 (1996): 473–86.

Frewer, L. J., C. Howard, and R. Shepherd. "Genetic Engineering and Food: What Determines Consumer Acceptance." *British Food Journal* 97 (1995): 31–36.

Frewer, L. J., C. Howard, and R. Shepherd. "Effective Communication about Genetic Engineering and Food." *British Food Journal* 98:415 (1996): 48–52.

Frewer, L. J., and R. Shepherd. "Attributing Information to Different Sources: Effects on the Perceived Qualities of Information, on the Perceived Relevance of Information, and on Attitude Formation." *Public Understanding Science* 3 (1994): 385–401.

Frewer, L. J., R. Shepherd, and P. Sparks. "Biotechnology and Food Production: Knowledge and Perceived Risk." *British Food Journal* 96 (1994): 26–32.

Gengler, C. E., D. J. Howard, and K. Zolner. "A Personal Construct Analysis of Adaptive Selling and Sales Experience." *Psychology and Marketing* 12:4 (1995): 287–304.

Gladston, I. "Motivation in Health Education." *Journal of the American Dietetic Association* 25 (1941): 745–51.

Gutman, J. "A Means-End Chain Model Based on Consumer Categorization Process." *Journal of Marketing* 42 (1982): 60–72.

Hadfield, G., R. Howse, and M. J. Trebilcock. *Rethinking Consumer Protection Policy.* Toronto: University of Toronto, Faculty of Law, Centre for the Study of State and Market Working Paper, 1996.

Hadfield, G., R. Howse, and M. J. Trebilcock. "Information-Based Principles: Biotechnology Is Influenced Not Only by Their Perceptions about the Magnitude for Rethinking Consumer Protection Policy." *Journal of Consumer Policy* 21 (1998): 131–69.

Hamstra, A. M. *Consumer Acceptance Model for Food Biotechnology: Final Report.* The Hague: The SWOKA Institute, 1995.

HealthFocus. "2003 Trend Survey." Atlanta: HealthFocus. <http://www.healthfocus. net>.

Heijs, W. J. M., and C. J. H. Midden. *Biotechnology: Attitudes and Influencing Factors, Third Survey.* Eindhoven: Eindhoven University of Technology, 1995.

Heijs, W. J. M., C. J. H. Midden, and R. A. J. Drabbe. *Biotechnology: Attitudes and Influencing Factors.* Eindhoven: Eindhoven University of Technology, 1993.

Hirshleifer, J., and J. G. Riley. *The Analytics of Uncertainty and Information.* Cambridge: Cambridge University Press, 1992.

Hofstede, G. *Culture's Consequences: International Differences in Work-Related Values.* London: Sage, 1980.

Hofstede, G. "The Cultural Relativity of Organizational Practices and Theories." *Journal of International Business Studies* 14 (Fall 1983): 75–89.

Howe, P. E. "Regional Food Habits as Related to Food Acceptance," *First Session: The Problem of Food Acceptability. Supreme Headquarters of The Allied Expeditionary Forces,* 1945.

Hunt, P., and M. Hillsdon. "A Model for Change" from *Changing Eating and Exercise Behavior: A Handbook for Professionals.* London: Blackwell Science Ltd., 1996.

Jasanoff, S. "Bridging the Two Cultures of Risk Analysis." *Risk Analysis* 13 (1993): 123–29.

Kahkonen, P., and H. Tuorila. "Effect of Reduced-Fat Information on Expected and Actual Hedonic and Sensory Ratings of Sausage." *Appetite* 30:1 (1998): 13–23.

Kahn, B. E., and B. Wansink. "The Influence of Assortment Structure on Perceived Variety and Consumption Quantities." *Journal of Consumer Research* 30:4 (March 2004).

Kapferer, J.-N., and G. Laurent. "Further Evidence on the Consumer Involvement Profile: Five Antecedents of Involvement." *Psychology & Marketing* 10 (July–August 1993): 347–55.

Kennedy, B. M. "Food Habits in California." *Fifth Session: Regional vs. National Food Habits and Nutrition,* Committee on Food Habits (mimeographed), 1945.

Kepner, K. W., R. D. Knutson, and J. P. Nichols. *Yogurt, Frozen Yogurt (Soft Serve), and Hard Frozen Yogurt Marketing Profile.* Washington, D.C.: American Cultured Dairy Products Institute, 1978.

Kuznesof, S., and C. Ritson. "Consumer Acceptability of Genetically Modified Foods with Special Reference to Farmed Salmon." *British Food Journal* 98:415 (1996): 39–47.

Lemkow, L. *Public Attitudes to Genetic Engineering: Some European Perspectives.* Dublin: Loughlinstown House, 1993.

Lewin, K. *Field Theory in Social Science: Selected Theoretical Papers.* New York: Harper & Row, 1951.

MacCrimmon, K. R., and D. A. Wehrung. *Taking Risks: The Management of Uncertainties.* New York: The Free Press, 1986.

Mead, M. "The Factor of Food Habits." *The Annals of the American Academy of Political and Social Science* (January 1943): 21–57.

Mela, D. J. "Food Choice and Intake: The Human Factor." *Proceedings of the Nutrition Society* 58:3 (1999): 513–21.

Miller, D. L. *Introduction to Collective Behavior.* Belmont, Calif.: Wadsworth, 1985.

Miller, D. L., V. H. Castellanos, D. J. Shide, J. C. Peters, and B. Rolls. "Effect of Fat-Free Potato Chips with and without Nutritional Labels on Fat and Energy Intakes." *The American Journal of Clinical Nutrition* 68 (1998): 282–90.

Modan, B., M. Tirosh, E. Weissenberg, C. Acker, T. Swartz, C. Coston, A. Donagi, M. Revach, and G. Vettorazzi. "The Arjenyattah Epidemic." *Lancet* 2 (1983): 1472–76.

Nasse, L. "Modeling the Future Acceptance of Soy Products." Unpublished master's thesis, University of Illinois at Urbana-Champaign, 2001.

National Institute of Mental Health. NIH Publication No. 95–3509, Revised 1995.

NPD Group. "17th Annual National Eating Trends Report." Port Washington, N.Y.: NPD Group, 2003. <http://www.NPDFoodWorld.com>.

Optima Consultants. *Understanding the Consumer Interest in the New Biotechnology Industry.* Ottawa: Industry Canada, 1994.

Painter, J. E., B. Wansink, and J. B. Hieggelke. "How Visibility and Convenience Influence Candy Consumption." *Appetite* 38:3 (June 2002): 237–38.

Patten, M. *Post-War Kitchen: Nostalgic Food and Facts from 1945–1954.* London: Hamlyn Reed Consumer Books Limited, 1998.

Pennings, J. M. E., and P. Garcia. "Measuring Producers' Risk Preferences: A Global

Risk Attitude Construct." *American Journal of Agricultural Economics* 83 (November 2001): 993–1009.

Pennings, J. M. E., and B. Wansink. "Channel Contract Behavior: The Role of Risk Attitudes, Risk Perceptions, and Channel Member Market Structures." *Journal of Business* (2005).

Pennings, J. M. E., B. Wansink, and M. M. E. Meulenberg. "A Note on Modeling Consumer Reactions to a Crisis: The Case of the Madcow Disease." *International Journal of Research in Marketing* 19:2 (March 2002): 91–100.

Petty, R. E., and J. T. Cacioppo. *Attitudes and Persuasion: Classic and Contemporary Approaches*. Dubuque, Iowa: Brown, 1981.

Petty, R. E., and J. T. Cacioppo. *Communication and Persuasion: Central and Peripheral Routes to Attitude Change*. New York: Springer-Verlag, 1986.

Philen, R. M., E. M. Kilbourn, and T. W. McKinley. "Mass Sociogenic Illness by Proxy: Parentally Reported in an Elementary School." *Lancet* 2 (1989): 1372–76.

Raats, M. M., R. Shepherd, and P. Sparks. "Including Moral Dimensions of Choice within the Structure of the Theory of Planned Behavior." *Journal of Applied Social Psychology* 25 (1995): 484–94.

Radke, M., and E. K. Caso. "Lecture and Discussion-Decision as Methods of Influencing Food Habits." *Journal of The American Dietetic Association* 24 (January 1948): 23–31.

Radke, M., and D. Klisurich. "Experiments in Changing Food Habits." *Journal of the American Dietetic Association* 23 (May 1947): 403–9.

Radovanovic, Z. "On the Origin of Mass Casualty Incidents in Kosovo, Yugoslavia, in 1990." *European Journal of Epidemiology* 11 (1995): 1–13.

Reynolds, T. J., and J. Gutman. "Laddering Theory, Method, Analysis, and Interpretation." *Journal of Advertising Research* (February/March 1988): 11–31.

Roberts, M. "A Consumer View of Biotechnology." *Consumer Policy Review* 4 (1994): 99–104.

Rolls, B. *Volumetrics*. New York: McGraw-Hill, 2003.

Rolls, B., and R. A. Barnett. *The Volumetrics Weight Control Plan*. New York: Harper-Collins, 2000.

Schoemaker, P. J. H. "The Expected Utility Model: Its Variants, Purposes, Evidence and Limitations." *Journal of Economic Literature* 20 (June 1982): 529–63.

Sheehy, H., M. Legault, and D. Ireland. "Consumer and Biotechnology: A Synopsis of Survey and Focus Group Research." *Journal of Consumer Policy* 21 (1998): 359–86.

Shide, D. J., and B. J. Rolls. "Information about Fat Content of Preloads Influences Energy Intake in Healthy Women." *Journal of the American Dietetic Association* 95 (1995): 993–98.

Shork, D. "A Matter of Taste: How Soyaworld Captured 60% of the Dairy Alternative Market." *Marketing (Maclean Hunter)* 105:20 (2000): 14.

Sjoberg, L., and B. M. Drottz-Sioberg. *Risk Perception of Nuclear Waste: Experts and the Public*. Report No. 16, Stockholm School of Economics, 1994.

Sloan, A. E. "What, When, and Where Americans Eat: 2003." *Food Technology* 57:8 (August 2003): 48–66.

Slovic, P. "Perceived Risk, Trust and Democracy." *Risk Analysis* 13 (1993): 675–82.

Slovic, P. "Perception of Risk." *Science* 236 (April 1987): 280–85.

Smelser, N. *Theory of Collective Behavior.* New York: Free Press, 1962.

Smith, M. E., E. O. van Ravenswaay, and S. R. Thompson. "Sales Loss Determination in Food Contamination Incidents: An Application to Milk Bans in Hawaii." *American Journal of Agricultural Economics* 70 (1988): 513–20.

Sparks, P., C. A. Guthrie, and R. Shepherd. "Perceived Behavioral Control or Perceived Behavioral Difficulty: Where's the Problem?" *Proceedings of the British Psychology Society* 4:1 (1995): 54.

Sparks, P., R. Shepherd, and L. J. Frewer. "Gene Technology, Food Production, and Public Opinion: A UK Study." *Agriculture and Human Values* 11:1 (1995): 19–28.

Sparks, P., R. Shepherd, and L. J. Frewer. "Assessing and Structuring Attitudes towards the Use of Gene Technology in Food Production: The Role of Perceived Ethical Obligation." *Basic and Applied Social Psychology* 16 (1995): 267–85.

Straughan, R. "Genetic Manipulation for Food Production: Social and Ethical Issues for Consumers." *British Food Journal* 92 (1991): 13–26.

Stubenitsky, K., J. I. Aaron, S. L. Catt, and D. J. Mela. "Effect of Information and Extended Use on the Acceptance of Reduced-Fat Products." *Food Quality and Preference* 10:4–5 (1999): 367–76.

Tait, J. "Public Perceptions of Biotechnology Hazards." *Journal of Chemical Technology and Biotechnology* 43 (1988): 363–72.

Tesser, A., and D. Shaffer. "Attitudes and Attitude Change." *Annual Review of Psychology* 41 (1990): 479–523.

Tuorila, H. M., H. L. Meiselman, A. V. Cardello, and L. L. Lesher. "Effect of Expectations and The Definition of Product Category on Acceptance of Unfamiliar Foods." *Food Quality and Preference* 9:6 (1998): 421–30.

Tversky, A., and D. Kahneman. "The Framing of Decisions and the Rationality of Choice." *Science* 211 (January 1981): 453–58.

van Ravenswaay, E. O., and J. P. Hoehn. "The Impact of Health Risk Information on Food Demand: A Case Study of Alar and Apples." In *Economics of Food Safety.* Ed. J. A. Caswell. 155–74. New York: Elsevier, 1991.

Wadman, M. "Agencies Face Uphill Battle to Keep United States Free of BSE." *Nature* 409 (January 2001): 441–42.

Wandel, M., and A. Bugge. "Consumer Valuation of Food Quality." *Appetite* 24:2 (1995): 198.

Wandel, M., and A. Bugge. "Environmental Concern in Consumer Evaluation of Food Quality." *Food Quality and Preference* 8 (1997): 19–26.

Wansink, B. "Advertising's Impact on Category Substitution." *Journal of Marketing Research* 31:4 (November 1994a): 505–15.

Wansink, B. "Antecedents and Mediators of Eating Bouts." *Family and Consumer Sciences Research Journal* 23:2 (December 1994b): 166–82.

Wansink, B. "Developing and Validating Useful Consumer Prototypes." *Journal of Targeting, Measurement and Analysis for Marketing* 3:1 (1994c): 18–30.

Wansink, B. "Can Package Size Accelerate Usage Volume?" *Journal of Marketing* 60:3 (July 1996): 1–14.

Wansink, B. "Developing Accurate Customer Usage Profiles." In *Values, Lifestyles, and Psychographics.* Ed. Lynn Kahle. 183–98. Cambridge, Mass.: Lexington, 1997.

Wansink, B. "Making Old Brands New." *American Demographics* 19:12 (December 1997): 53–58.

Wansink, B. "New Techniques to Generate Key Marketing Insights." *Marketing Research* (Summer 2000): 28–36.

Wansink, B. "Changing Eating Habits on the Home Front: Lost Lessons from World War II Research." *Journal of Public Policy and Marketing* 21:1 (Spring 2002): 90–99.

Wansink, B. "Do Front and Back Package Labels Influence Beliefs about Health Claims?" *Journal of Consumer Affairs* 37:2 (December 2003a).

Wansink, B. "Overcoming the Taste Stigma of Soy." *Journal of Food Science* (September 2003b).

Wansink, B. "Point-of-Purchase Advertising." In *Encyclopedia of Advertising.* Ed. John McDonough and Karen Egolf. 1243–45. New York: Fitzroy Dearborn, 2003c.

Wansink, B. "Profiling Nutritional Gatekeepers: Three Methods for Differentiating Influential Cooks." *Food Quality and Preference* 14:4 (June 2003d): 289–97.

Wansink, B. "Using Laddering to Understand and Leverage a Brand's Equity." *Qualitative Market Research: An International Journal* 6:2 (2003e): 111–18.

Wansink, B. "Vegemite." In *Encyclopedia of Advertising.* Ed. John McDonough and Karen Egolf. 1603–4. New York: Fitzroy Dearborn, 2003f.

Wansink, B. "Food Marketing." In *Encyclopedia of American Food and Drink.* Ed. A. F. Smith. New York: Oxford University Press, 2004.

Wansink, B., and N. Chan. "Relation of Soy Consumption to Nutritional Knowledge." *Journal of Medicinal Foods* 4:3 (December 2001): 147–52.

Wansink, B., M. M. Cheney, and N. Chan. "Understanding Comfort Food Preferences across Gender and Age." *Physiology and Behavior* 53:8 (2004).

Wansink, B., and J. Cheong. "Taste Profiles That Correlate with Soy Consumption in Developing Countries." *Pakistan Journal of Nutrition* 1:6 (December 2002): 276–78.

Wansink, B., and J. Kim. "The Marketing Battle over Genetically Modified Foods: False Assumptions about Consumer Behavior." *American Behavioral Scientist* 44:8 (April 2001): 1405–17.

Wansink, B., J. M. Painter, and K. van Ittersum. "Descriptive Menu Labels' Effect on Sales." *Cornell Hotel and Restaurant Administrative Quarterly* 42:6 (December 2001): 68–72.

Wansink, B., and S.-B. Park. "Accounting for Taste: Prototypes That Predict Preference." *Journal of Database Marketing* 7:4 (2000): 308–20.

Wansink, B., and S.-B. Park. "Methods and Measures That Profile Heavy Users." *Journal of Advertising Research* 40:4 (July–August 2000): 61–72.

Wansink, B., and S.-B. Park. "At the Movies: How External Cues and Perceived Taste Impact Consumption Volume." *Food Quality and Preference* 12:1 (January 2001): 69–74.

Wansink, B., and S.-B. Park. "Sensory Suggestiveness and Labeling: Do Soy Labels Bias Taste?" *Journal of Sensory Studies* 17:5 (November 2002): 483–91.

Wansink, B., S.-B. Park, S. Sonka, and M. Morganosky. "How Soy Labeling Influences Preference and Taste." *International Food and Agribusiness Management Review* 3 (2000): 85–94.

Wansink, B., and M. L. Ray. "Advertising Strategies to Increase Usage Frequency." *Journal of Marketing* 60:1 (January 1996): 31–46.

Wansink, B., M. L. Ray, and R. Batra. "Increasing Cognitive Response Sensitivity." *Journal of Advertising* 23:2 (June 1994): 65–75.

Wansink, B., and C. Sangerman. "Engineering Comfort Foods." *American Demographics* (July 2000): 66–67.

Wansink, B., S. T. Sonka, and M. M. Cheney. "A Cultural Hedonic Framework for Increasing the Consumption of Unfamiliar Foods: Soy Acceptance in Russia and Columbia." *Review of Agricultural Economics* 24:2 (2002): 353–65.

Wansink, B., S. T. Sonka, J. Chirbogi, P. Goldsmith, and N. Eren. "International Best Practices in Marketing Soy," *Journal of International Food and Agribusiness Marketing* (July 2004).

Wansink, B., and R. E. Westgren. "Profiling Taste-Motivated Segments." *Appetite*, 41 (2004): 323–27.

Wildavsky, A., and K. Dake. "Theories of Risk Perception: Who Fears What and Why?" *Daedalus* 119 (1990): 41–60.

Wilson, I. S. "Share the Meat," *What's New in Food and Nutrition* 1:2 (1943): 26–39.

Wohl, J. B. "Consumers' Decision-Making and Risk Perceptions Regarding Foods Produced with Biotechnology." *Journal of Consumer Policy* 21 (1998): 387–404.

Wright, L. T., C. Nancarrow, and P. M. H. Kwok. "Food Taste Preferences and Cultural Influences on Consumption." *British Food Journal* 103:2 (2001): 348–57.

Young, E. "If Sheep Get BSE from Blood, Why Can't People?" *New Scientist* 167:2257 (September 2000): 6.

Zellner, D. A., C. E. Tornow, and R. F. Winitch. "Expectations Can Produce Hedonic Contrast." In *Fechner Day 92*. Ed. G. Borg and G. Neely. 229–34. Stockholm: Stockholm University, 1992.

Index

Brian Wansink (Ph.D., Stanford University, 1990) is professor of applied economics and management, of marketing, and of nutritional science at Cornell University, formerly the Julian Simon Faculty Scholar and a professor of marketing, nutritional science, and agricultural and consumer economics at the University of Illinois at Urbana-Champaign. His research expertise is in marketing nutrition and in how and why marketing-related variables influence the selection and overeating of food (<www.FoodPsychology.com>). He has published more than a hundred journal articles and has coauthored *Consumer Panels* and *Asking Questions*. In 1999 he founded the Consumer Education Foundation, a nonprofit organization that helps people become more responsible consumers.

The Food Series

A History of Cooking   *Michael Symons*
Peanuts: The Illustrious History of the Goober Pea   *Andrew F. Smith*
Marketing Nutrition: Soy, Functional Foods, Biotechnology,
    and Obesity   *Brian Wansink*
The Banquet: Dining in the Great Courts of Late Renaissance
    Ken Albala
The Turkey: An American Story   *Andrew F. Smith*
The Herbaliist in the Kitchen   *Gary Allen*

The University of Illinois Press
is a founding member of the
Association of American University Presses.

Composed in 9.5/13 ITC Stone Serif
with ITC Stone Sans display
by Jim Proefrock
at the University of Illinois Press
Designed by Paula Newcomb

University of Illinois Press
1325 South Oak Street
Champaign, IL 61820-6903
www.press.uillinois.edu